Contents

Credits

Authors and editors of this book

Andrew Hunt
Nicholas Russell

Contributors

Bruce Allen
John Beeby
Brian Bell
Chris Boothroyd
Colin Butler
Geraldine Duggan

David Evans
Graham Harris
Fran Hopwood
Sherry Husselbury
John Lawton
Trevor Lund

Steve Lewis
John Main
Jane Morris
Cris Rainbow
Andrew Rankin
Vince Scannella

Ian Smith
Rosemary Taylor
Angela Turner
Anna Wheadon
Raymond Whiteford

Project management committee

Lindsey Charles   Heinemann Education
Andrew Hunt   Director
Nicholas Russell   Deputy director
Anthony Tomei   Nuffield Foundation
Linda Westgarth   Administrator

Regional working groups

North west

Blackpool and the Fylde College
Bolton College
Bury College
Macclesfield College
The Nelson Thomlinson School
St Chads RC Comprehensive School
St Helens College
The Ridge College
Weatherhead High School
Wigan and Leigh College

North east

Acklam College
Ashington High School
Hirst High School
Northumberland College
Newcastle College
Prudhoe County High School

North central

Airedale and Wharfedale College
Barnsley College
Calderdale College
Hanson School
Hull College
John Leggott College
Leeds College of Technology
Wakefield College
Woodkirk High School

Midlands

Coventry Technical College
Darlaston Community School
Halesowen College
North East Worcestershire College
Matthew Boulton College
North Birmingham College
North Nottinghamshire College
Peterborough College
Sandwell College
St Augustine's School
The City Technology College,
   Kingshurst
Walsall College

South west

Gorseinon College
Plymouth College of Further
   Education
St Brendan's Sixth Form College
Thomas Hardy School, Dorchester
Weymouth College
Yeovil College

South east

Amersham and Wycombe College
Bedford College
Brooklands College
Castle High School
Chelmsford College

Christ the King Sixth Form College
Esher College
Farnborough Sixth Form College
Godalming College
Greenhill College
Greenford High School
Hackney Community College
Henley College
Hertford Regional College
Islington Sixth Form Centre
Kingsbury High School
Kingston College
Lord Grey School
Luton Sixth Form College
Merton Sixth Form College
Oxford College of Further Education
Spelthorne College
Stantonbury Campus
The College of North East London
The North School, Ashford
Woking College
Uplands Community School

We are very grateful to Jim Breithaupt (NW), Robert Peers (NE), Stuart
Charlton and Geoffrey Gardner (NC), Colin Butler (M) and Derek Bodey (SW)
for their help with organizing the meetings of these groups.

NUFFIELD SCIENCE *in* PRACTICE

GNVQ SCIENCE

Your questions answered

AN INTRODUCTION AND GUIDE TO GNVQ SCIENCE

Heinemann

Heinemann Educational Publishers
a division of Heinemann Publishers (Oxford) Ltd,
Halley Court, Jordan HIll, Oxford, OX2 8EJ

OXFORD   LONDON   EDINBURGH
MADRID   ATHENS   BOLOGNA   PARIS
MELBOURNE   SYDNEY   AUCKLAND   SINGAPORE   TOKYO
IBADAN   NAIROBI   HARARE   GABORONE
PORTSMOUTH NH (USA)

First published 1994

97 96 95 94
10 9 8 7 6 5 4 3 2 1

ISBN 0 435 63256 6

Designed and typeset by Gecko Ltd, Bicester, Oxon

Illustrated by Gecko Limited and Pantelis Palios

Printed by Thomson Litho, Scotland

Acknowledgements

The authors and publishers would like to thank the following for permission to use copyright
material:

© NCVQ for the extract taken from *Advanced Mandatory Unit* 3 on p.10; Business &
Technology Education Council (BTEC) for the extract taken from the *Catering
Occupational Standards Level 1* on p.15; Crown Copyright for the two extracts taken
from Government White Papers: *Education and Training in the 21st Century 1991* and
Generic Competencie; 1991 on p.11 and p.14. Reproduced with the permission of the
Controller of Her Majesty's Stationery Office. Further Education Unit for the following two
extracts: *Learning by Doing* FEU 1988 on p.89 and *A Guide to Teaching and Learning
Methods* by Graham Gibbs taken from *Learning by Doing* FEU 1987 on pp.96–7;
HarperCollins Publishers for the two extracts taken from *Active Teaching and Learning
in Science* by Hallam University on p.87 and p.90; Peter Honey for the extract taken from
The Manual of Learning Styles-1992-3rd Edition on pp.94–5; IOP Publishing Ltd. for the
extract taken from *Physics Education* (article by John Sparks) on pp.85–6; New Scientist
for the article *Playtime for Postgrads* by Kate Douglas on p.95; Dr. David Tyrrell for his
interview on p.86.

The Publishers have made every effort to trace the copyright holders, but if they have
inadvertently overlooked any, they will be pleased to make the necessary arrangements at
the first opportunity.

Nuffield Science in Practice

Nuffield Science in Practice is a curriculum development project funded by the Nuffield Foundation. We have a small central team but most of our work is done by teachers and lecturers all over the country.

Since the early summer of 1993, we have been working with staff from many GNVQ pilot centres in six regional groups. The groups meet once or twice a term. Staff have also attended from other colleges and schools planning to embark on GNVQ Science in September 1994.

Most of the advice and information in this guide is based on what we have learnt from these meetings. We have also included a series of case studies to give a feeling for what GNVQ Science is actually like. The case studies show that the GNVQ specification is flexible enough to allow great variety in vocational science programmes.

All the case studies in chapters 3 to 6 were written by lecturers and teachers in colleges and schools. There are lots of them and the first time you read this book you may want to skip over some of them. Brief introductions will help you identify the examples which are related to your interests.

We commissioned the two case studies in chapter 9. They are therefore written from the point of a sympathetic outsider visiting the school or college to interview staff and students. These studies include reflections on the strengths and weaknesses of GNVQ with discussion of useful lessons for newcomers to vocational science programmes.

Figure 1.1
Map of the UK showing the
location of regional groups

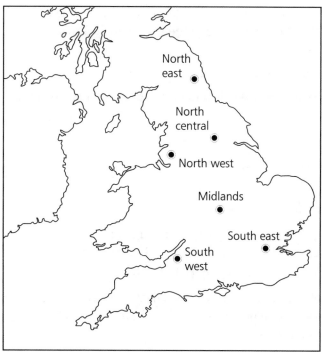

A feature of our project meetings is the frankness with which the participants describe their experiences with GNVQ Science. In a similar way the contributors to this book are very open about their courses. All the case studies are authentic but we agreed not to identify the centres to make it easier for the authors to describe their difficulties as well as their successes.

We hope this book will answer most of your questions about GNVQ Science. Writing at the end of the first term of the pilot year, we cannot offer 'right' answers but we hope the advice from our collaborators will complement the guidance from awarding bodies. We also hope to reassure those embarking on GNVQ Science that they will survive the trip, albeit after a challenging and, possibly bumpy, ride.

There are some questions which it is too early to answer: important questions about the standards, grading of GNVQ and the acceptability of the new qualification to employers and higher education. We hope to be able to offer guidance on these issues once pilot centres have had more experience with their new programmes.

'Go for it – but get organized early on.'

Finally a comment on the quotations which appear from time to time in the margins in this book. They come from lecturers and teachers who replied to this question: 'If you could give one piece of advice to centres starting GNVQ for the first time, what would you say to them?'.

Project publications

This book is the first of a series of publications to support colleges and schools offering GNVQ Science from September 1994. Our initial publication programme covers the mandatory units.

Publications in 1994

In the summer of 1994 we will publish two photocopiable files of assignments – one for Intermediate level and one for Advanced level. Each file will include:

- unit study guides – a set of short tasks which will help students build up notes to cover the range in sufficient depth for the end-of-module tests
- outline assignments – ideas for assignments for pilot centres with details of the student tasks and references to resources
- fully elaborated assignments – complete with notes for staff, task sheets, information and practical guidance
- a map of other resources – this will match published resources to the elements, performance criteria and ranges of the GNVQ units.

We will publish a students' book for the Intermediate course in summer 1994. The book will:

- set the GNVQ specification in context by featuring studies which illustrate how people who use science in their work fulfil GNVQ performance criteria
- explore some wider aspects of working with science
- provide basic coverage of knowledge and understanding specified in the element ranges
- act as a reference book, including a data section
- provide opportunities to develop core skills.

Publications in 1995

We will publish further batches of assignments to supplement the earlier files. We will also publish a GNVQ Science Advanced students' book covering all the mandatory units and with similar aims to the Intermediate text.

NCVQ will announce changes to the GNVQ specification in 1994. Our student publications will not be published until we have checked that they match the revised mandatory units.

General National Vocational Qualifications

In the beginning

We have written this book for science teachers and lecturers in schools, sixth form and further education colleges who find themselves in any of the following situations.

- You have heard of GNVQs and want to discover more.

- You feel that GNVQ might suit students who are not coping well with traditional A level.

- You are unhappy with the rigid teaching framework of A level. You have heard that GNVQ might be a more flexible way to teach.

- Your senior managers have decided that GNVQs are a good thing. Your department has been told to introduce them.

- You have been running vocational courses for some time, probably BTEC First or National Diploma, but you have learned that they will be replaced by GNVQ.

You have probably made contact with one of the three bodies who award GNVQs, the Royal Society of Arts (RSA), the Business and Technology Education Council (BTEC) or the City and Guilds of London Institute (CGLI). Their literature describes GNVQs in detail and defines the assessment procedures, but the language is rather daunting and the conceptual basis of GNVQ is complicated. What you need is a very simple outline of how GNVQ works.

This is also what potential students need to help them to decide whether GNVQ is the qualification they want and to introduce them to the course. There follows an example of a student's guide to GNVQ, distilled from a number of introductory leaflets produced by pilot schools and colleges. It should provide you with all the basic things you need to know about GNVQ now and can be used as a framework for developing your own introductory student material. We will publish photocopiable versions of this guide in our files of assignments.

1 The qualification of the future

GNVQs are new qualifications. GNVQs in science are based on what scientists and engineers actually do in their jobs, rather than on academic subject areas. They are strongly backed by the government and employers and when you achieve your GNVQ you will have a valuable qualification, whether you want to go straight into employment or decide to go on to university.

On a GNVQ course you will:

- 'learn by doing' through a wide variety of activities (such as carrying out experiments, taking part in discussions, role-plays and debates, carrying out research from books, magazines and videos, doing calculations, writing reports, going on visits, making presentations and responding to questions)

- take considerable responsibility for your own learning and

- be assessed on your skills and achievements as you work through the course.

2 Course structure

GNVQs are modular courses, which means that they are split up into separate units. At present, GNVQ can be studied at two levels, Intermediate and Advanced.

- At Intermediate level, GNVQ will normally take a single academic year to complete and consists of 4 mandatory (compulsory) units of work, 2 optional units (from a choice of 4) and 3 units of core skills. This level is for students with good GCSE results, but few A–C grades. The completed GNVQ Intermediate qualification is equivalent to 4 GCSE passes at grade C or above.

- Advanced GNVQ will normally take two academic years to complete and consists of 8 mandatory (compulsory) units, 4 optional units and 3 units of core skills. This level is for students who have 4 or more GCSEs at grade C or above. The Advanced GNVQ is equivalent to two A level passes and is therefore acceptable as a basic qualification for university entrance.

3 Learning and assessment

During the course you will carry out a series of tasks and activities, set for you by the GNVQ course team. These tasks are grouped into assignments through which you will both learn science and produce evidence that you have mastered all parts of each unit. The evidence will take the form of a portfolio of coursework. We will discuss the standard of your work with as you build your portfolio.

For the mandatory units you will also have to pass unit tests. The pass mark for these is high (70%) but you can retake the tests if you fail. Although you must pass a test to obtain a pass in that unit, the result does not count towards the grading of your achievement. Each unit test will be straightforward and last for one hour.

Each unit is broken down into elements which tell you what you have to do to pass the unit. We assess your work in each element with the help of performance criteria. These are statements which make it clear what the element is about. The performance criteria must be met and we have to make sure that you have a chance to tackle every one. You have to carry out tasks in a range of situations before you can be awarded the unit.

In addition to the science units, GNVQ requires that you acquire other, more general, core skills. These are assessed in three areas, communication, numeracy and information technology. You will have opportunities to learn and develop these skills with specialist staff, but your performance will be assessed when you use these skills in your science assignment coursework.

4 The qualifications and their grading

At the end of the course you will receive a certificate listing all the units you have completed successfully. At Intermediate level, if you complete all 9 units, you will achieve a GNVQ Intermediate pass. At Advanced level, 15 units are needed for a pass. You may be awarded a merit or distinction grade if your completed portfolio of coursework assignments shows that you have performed particularly well in the following areas.

Planning — how you plan your work so that all tasks are completed within the deadline, how you cope with difficulties and how you monitor your progress.

Gathering and using information — how you select and handle information, that your research is as extensive as possible within available limits and how you process information from a variety of sources.

Evaluation (at Advanced level only) — how you judge the success of your plan of action and identify other ways that could have been or were considered in reaching your conclusions.

5 What we will provide

We will ensure that you cover all the elements of all the units. Your day-to-day work will take the form of assignments which ask you to complete certain tasks.

The tasks are activities designed to give you opportunities to show and improve the range of your knowledge and skills in science units and the three core-skill units.

By completing the assignments successfully and within deadlines we guarantee that you will accumulate all the necessary evidence needed to show that you have reached the appropriate GNVQ level.

6 What we expect from you

You have to show us your ability to work in a scientific manner in a variety of activities across all areas of science. This is a demanding course because so much is left to you to organize and plan your own work. You are responsible for the day-to-day completion of your tasks and for ensuring that they are completed within the agreed deadlines.

We expect you to complete your assignments to a high academic and technical standard and to present them professionally. We expect you to collect the evidence of your achievements in the various elements and assemble it into a portfolio. The portfolio must be organized and cross-referenced so that your tutors and any verifiers can see exactly where to find the evidence that you have met all the performance criteria for every element in each unit.

7 Who is who in the delivery of GNVQs?

■ **The centre co-ordinator**
The person in the school or college responsible for overseeing the operation of GNVQs.

■ **The programme co-ordinators**
The tutors in the school or college responsible for particular GNVQ courses.

■ **Assessors**
The staff responsible for assessing your work. All programme deliverers are assessors.

■ **Internal verifier**
The person in the school or college responsible for monitoring the work of all GNVQ students and checking that all the assessors are marking assignments to the same standards.

■ **External verifier**
A person appointed by the awarding body (RSA, BTEC or City and Guilds) to make sure the school or college is teaching GNVQs properly. From time to time the external verifier will come to meet all the tutors and students involved.

8 Finally

The course team will help you in every possible way in all aspects of the course. Please feel free to talk over any problems or suggestions you may have with any of your course tutors who will be more than happy to help.

The detailed structure of GNVQ specifications

Now let us look at the detailed unit specifications. Consider the mandatory science units which all students must do. The frontsheet carries a list of four (Intermediate) or eight (Advanced) units. Each unit has three or more subtitles, all of which begin with active verbs such as 'carry out', 'prepare', 'monitor', 'manage' or 'investigate'. The specifications for the pilot year look like this (part of Advanced mandatory unit 3).

Figure 2.1

UNIT 3: OBTAIN NEW SUBSTANCES (ADVANCED)

Element 3.1: Plan the preparation of a substance

Performance criteria

1 the substance to be made is identified
2 possible preparative routes to obtain the substance are identified
3 the selected route is justified

Range   **Substances:** elements, compounds (inorganic, organic, biologically important)
Preparative routes: single and multi-step conversions; acid–base, redox, substitution, elimination, addition
Selection criteria: availability of starting materials, feasibility of conversion, cost

Evidence indicators

Reports recommending preparative routes to at least two different substances, of which one should be inorganic and the other organic. In each case, the reports should compare and contrast possible routes and justify the choice of the one which is recommended. Between them, the preparative routes should include reactions from a minimum of three of the following general categories: acid–base, redox, substitution, elimination, addition.
Evidence will also show that the candidate understands the performance criteria in relation to all the items in the range. The unit test will confirm the candidate's coverage of range.

Element 3.2: Prepare an amount of substance

Performance criteria

1 the quantity of substance to be made is specified
2 a preparative reaction is identified
3 quantities of reactants required are calculated
4 potential hazards are identified
5 preparation is carried out
6 safety procedures are carried out
7 factors to be considered when scaling up the reaction are identified

Range   **Substances:** elements, compounds (inorganic, organic, biologically important)
Quantity: laboratory scale, production scale
Calculations: amounts of substance, mole ratio, balanced chemical equations
Preparative reactions: acid–base, redox, substitution, elimination, addition
Factors: apparatus, transfer of material, heating
Safety: site procedures, COSHH, HASAWA, EC directives

Evidence indicators

Products from a minimum of three laboratory preparations. At least one product should be inorganic and one should be organic. Each preparation should require a different type of preparative reaction, to be taken from the following list: acid–base, redox, substitution, elimination, addition. Reports on factors to be considered when scaling up each of the three preparations should be produced.
Evidence will also show that the candidate understands the performance criteria in relation to all the items in the range. The unit test will confirm the candidate's coverage of range.

The subtitles from the frontsheet are repeated as **elements** and are followed by statements under three headings, **performance criteria**, **range** and **evidence indicators**.

Why are the specifications written in this way and what do they mean?

Training, not education

In 1986 the government published a White Paper, *Working together, Education and Training*, which pointed out that the training and education of the British workforce was inadequate. The National Council for Vocational Qualifications (NCVQ) was set up to do something about it.

NCVQ has two broad objectives: to standardize and improve the huge range of existing job-related training schemes and to spread the training message and the necessary qualifications into those parts of British industry and commerce which previous exhortations have failed to reach. The system adopted to achieve these goals is the National Vocational Qualification (NVQ).

NVQs provide a uniform framework of levels of competence for jobs, trades and professions, together with a set of assessment criteria against which the performance of trainees is compared to see if they are competent. The standards are laid down by representative practitioners of the trades and professions concerned, operating through industrial and commercial Lead Bodies. Statements of underpinning knowledge and understanding are then grafted onto the statements of practical competence.

In 1991 the government published another White Paper, *Education and Training in the 21st Century*, which re-emphasized the importance of vocational training. It endorsed a set of ambitious training targets, first proposed by industry, indicating what proportions of the British workforce should be trained to what levels of competence by the year 2000.

Figure 2.2

> ## NATIONAL TARGETS FOR EDUCATION AND TRAINING FOUNDATION LEARNING
>
> 1 By 1997, 80% of young people should reach NVQ level 2 (Intermediate) or the equivalent (i.e. GCSE with at least 4 passes at A–C grades).
> 2 Training and education to NVQ level 3 (Advanced) or the equivalent (2 A levels) should be available to all young people who can benefit.
> 3 By the year 2000, 50% of young people should reach NVQ level 3 (Advanced) or its equivalent.
> 4 There should be education and training provision for young people to develop self-reliance, flexibility and breadth.

The 1991 White Paper also proposed the introduction of General National Vocational Qualifications (GNVQs) as an alternative to A level study for 16–19 year olds still in full-time education. The primary aim of the new qualifications is to prepare students either for direct entry into a trade, or as an entry qualification for more vocational training or education at university.

The pattern for the new GNVQs is the same as for NVQs. But whereas NVQs are mainly about job-specific skills and competencies, GNVQs focus on the knowledge and understanding which underpin work in a broad employment sector, together with some more general skills.

The government has engineered a three track progression beyond the National Curriculum. Firstly, the academic route, via A and AS levels to degrees and higher degrees, secondly, a vocational route via work and work-related training, and thirdly a potentially uneasy compromise between the two systems, GNVQ, a nominally vocational qualification set in a full-time educational context (figure 2.3).

Since GNVQs are based on the NVQ framework, we will explain the structure of NVQs first.

Figure 2.3
NVQ, GNVQ and A levels post-16

	GNVQ	NVQ Level	Occupationally-specific NVQ	
	Vocationally-related Post Graduate qualifications	5	Professional qualification middle management	
Degree	Vocationally-related Degrees/ Higher National Diploma	4	Higher Technician. Junior Management	Degree
A/AS Level	GNVQ Advanced	3	Technician. Advanced Craft. Supervisor	A/AS Level
GCSE	GNVQ Intermediate	2	Basic Craft Certificate	GCSE
National Curriculum	GNVQ Foundation	1	Semi-skilled	National Curriculum

The NVQ framework

NVQs are qualifications about work, based on standards set by industry. NVQs set standards but they say nothing about how people acquire the skills and knowledge they need to meet those standards. There are no rules restricting access and people may prepare for an NVQ at work, at college or in their spare time.

Each NVQ is made up of a number of units, which set out the standards in statements of competence. The design of NVQ units is based on a particular description of competence which assumes that the main components of skills, knowledge and personal effectiveness are integrated to achieve work **outcomes**. Therefore, the focus is not on the performance of individual skills as such but on the achievement of an outcome or task which is to be performed.

Figure 2.4
Structure of NVQ qualifications

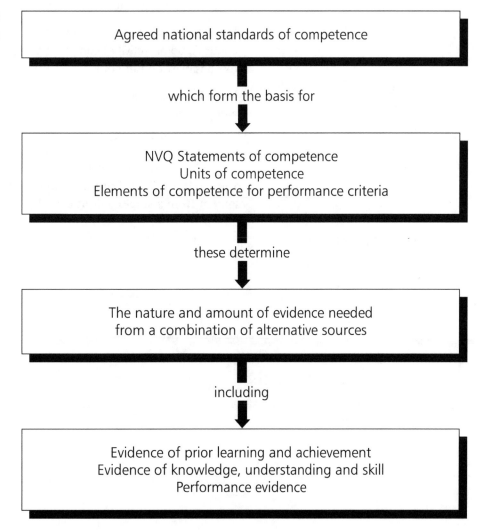

Agreed national standards of competence

which form the basis for

NVQ Statements of competence
Units of competence
Elements of competence for performance criteria

these determine

The nature and amount of evidence needed
from a combination of alternative sources

including

Evidence of prior learning and achievement
Evidence of knowledge, understanding and skill
Performance evidence

There are five levels in the NVQ framework of which level 1 is the simplest.

Figure 2.5

SUMMARIES OF THE GENERIC COMPETENCIES TO BE SHOWN AT THE FIVE NVQ LEVELS

level 5: competence in applying a range of fundamental principles and complex techniques across wide and unpredictable contexts. Substantial personal autonomy and often significant responsibility for the work of others and for the allocation of substantial resources.

level 4: competence in a broad range of of complex technical and professional activities performed in a wide variety of contexts with a substantial degree of personal responsibility and autonomy. Responsibility for the work of others and the allocation of resources is often present.

level 3: competence in a broad range of varied work performed in a variety of contexts, most of which are complex and non-routine. Considerable responsibility and autonomy, often with control or guidance of others.

level 2: competence in a significant range of varied work, in a variety of contexts. Some activities complex and non-routine, some individual responsibility or autonomy. Team collaboration may often be a requirement.

level 1: competence in the performance of a range of varied work, most of which is routine and predictable.

We can illustrate the typical structure of an NVQ with the help of an example from BTEC Catering and hospitality. Figure 2.6 shows one element from a single unit at level 1.

Figure 2.6

NVQ
PERFORMANCE CRITERION:
DINING FURNITURE IS
CLEAN AND READY
RANGE:
FOOD SERVICE AREA,
CUSTOMER DINING AREA,
DINING ITEMS, ASH
TRAYS...

Catering and Hospitality Industry and Licensed Trade: Occupational Standards for NVQs/SVQs Level 1

Key Role	C	Serve Food and Drinks to the Customer
Unit	1C3	Prepare and Clear Areas for Counter Service
Element	**1C3.3**	**Clear Dining and Service Areas after Food Service**

Performance Criteria

1) Re-usable dining items used in food service are assembled for cleaning or stored correctly.

2) Food items and accompaniments for future use are stored in accordance with food hygiene regulations.

3) Rubbish, used disposable and waste food are disposed of in accordance with food hygiene regulations.

4) Service equipment is clean and where appropriate turned off or stored.

5) Dining furniture is clean and ready for future use.

6) Dining and service areas are left tidy and ready for cleaning.

7) Unexpected situations are reported and dealt with in accordance with laid down procedures.

8) Work is carried out in accordance with laid down procedures.

9) Work is carried out within the required time.

Range

Food service areas:

- customer dining areas
- food counters and other service areas

Condiments and accompaniments:

- seasoning
- sugars and sweetners
- prepared sauces and dressings

Dining items:

- trays
- crockery or disposables
- cutlery or disposables
- glassware or disposables
- ashtrays

Service equipment:

- service utensils
- hot and cold beverage
- dispensers
- refrigerated units
- heated units
- display units
- food containers

Laid down procedures:

- all relevant health and safety legislation
- all relevant food hygiene legislation
- all relevant establishment procedures

Underpinning Knowledge Evidence:

- why all food service areas should be left clean after service.
- why certain electrical equipment should be turned off after service.
- why waste must be handled and disposed of correctly.

Assessment Methods

Evidence of competence to cover all of the performance criteria across the range must be assessed using one of the following methods:

A) Totally by observation in the workplace or realistic environment

B) Observation for a minimum of:

i) 2 from the range of food service areas
ii) 3 from the range of dining items
iii) 2 from the range of condiments and accompaniments
iv) 4 from the range of service equipment

Plus supplementary evidence in the form of:

a) Questioning which can be oral, using visual aids or technology based aids.

Evidence of underpinning knowledge must be assessed by questioning, which can be oral, using visual aids or technology based aids.

This is a detailed training schedule for junior operatives in the hotel and catering industries. The structure of units, elements, performance criteria, range and so on is obviously appropriate for training of this kind. The performance criteria are all about doing tasks and the range sets out the situations and equipment in and with which the tasks must be performed.

However, this is not a purely competence based programme. The junior trainees need some underpinning knowledge to enable them to carry out the performance criteria satisfactorily. They need to understand why they must carry out procedures in a certain way.

When the trainees (or their supervisors) gauge that they have enough experience and knowledge to be assessed, they are evaluated as they carry out the specified tasks by a trained assessor.

To make up a qualification, employees must prove competence in a mix of units appropriate for the roles for which they are training. Thus there is a profile of seven units for the achievement of a complete NVQ level 1 Catering and hospitality (serving food and drink counter). However, because the programme is modular, trainees can be given for credit for the units in which they have shown competence, even if they do not acquire a complete NVQ.

GNVQ specifications

GNVQ specifications have been modelled closely on the NVQ format. The main difference is that units and elements of **competence** are replaced by units and elements of **achievement**.

Figure 2.7

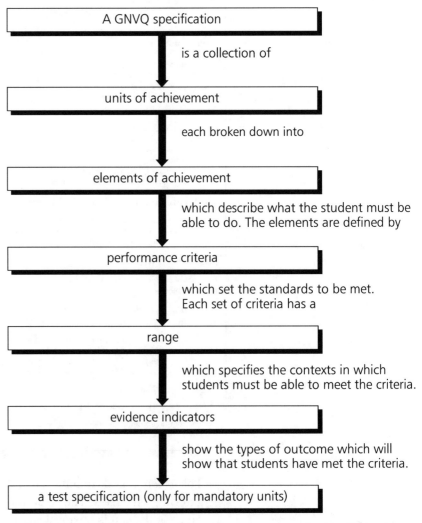

A GNVQ specification

is a collection of

units of achievement

each broken down into

elements of achievement

which describe what the student must be able to do. The elements are defined by

performance criteria

which set the standards to be met. Each set of criteria has a

range

which specifies the contexts in which students must be able to meet the criteria.

evidence indicators

show the types of outcome which will show that students have met the criteria.

a test specification (only for mandatory units)

shows how an external test will check coverage of the range in the spirit of the performance criteria.

GNVQ Science mandatory units
(in 1993/94)
Intermediate
unit 1 Work on scientific tasks
unit 2 Explore materials
unit 3 Make useful products
unit 4 Control systems

Advanced
unit 1 Analyse and identify substances and
        specimens
unit 2 Investigate materials and their use
unit 3 Obtain new substances
unit 4 Obtain products from living systems
unit 5 Energy transfer
unit 6 Control reactions
unit 7 Manage living systems
unit 8 Handle data in science

Optional units from RSA (in 1993/4)
Intermediate
Food science
Sports science
Forensic science
Earth science

Advanced
Ecology and land management
Environmental health
Biotechnology
Polymers for a purpose
Chemicals by design
Light and colour
Medical physics
Communication system

Optional units from BTEC (in 1993/4)
Intermediate
The nature of everyday change
Energy for the motor car
Investigating life
Earth science

Advanced
Chemical processes – how fast, how far?
Chemical processes – facts and reasons
Mathematics for science
Investigating physics applications
Electronic systems applied to scientific
measurement
Science and the environment
Micro-organisms and cells in biotechnology
Applied biotechnology

Optional units from City and Guilds
(in 1993/4)
Intermediate
Transport by air and sea
Food production
Health and fitness
Science for presentation and performance

Advanced
Transport
Giant molecules
Earth science
Communication and storage of data
The application and design of medicines
The body in action
Horticulture
Science of consumer products

Although all three awarding bodies accredit GNVQ Science, RSA was responsible for setting up the advisory and working groups which devised the mandatory units for GNVQ Science.

All awarding bodies use the RSA-generated mandatory unit specifications and the NCVQ-devised core-skill units. However, each awarding body

■ offers its own mandatory unit tests

■ its own range of optional units and

■ a distinctive menu of additional units.

Students who achieve at least one unit receive a certificate listing their achievements. Students who achieve the full award are eligible for 'merit' or 'distinction' grades. The grading **refers to the whole award**. Individual units are not graded.

The external knowledge tests check that students have achieved a basic mastery of the range. The tests are pitched at a level such that 80 per cent of the students can achieve a 70 per cent pass mark.

Students can take the tests again and again until they pass. For the pilots, the awarding bodies have arranged four testing sessions in the year. Machine-markable tests make it possible to get the results back to students rapidly so they know whether or not to re-enter for the next testing session.

Test results form no part of the grading or assessment of GNVQ. An analogy with the driving test helps to put the mandatory unit tests into perspective. Competent drivers pass the test if they satisfy the examiners that they are in control, have good road sense and are safe to let loose on their own (GNVQ assembly of a portfolio of evidence). But novice drivers also have to answer questions about the highway code to check that they have mastered the underpinning knowledge (GNVQ mandatory unit tests).

The notion of **grading** a portfolio of evidence is completely alien to the original NVQ culture, which is about assessing whether a candidate for an award can or cannot achieve the specifications for competence. For GNVQs, grading has been added to the NVQ framework largely to meet demands from Higher Education.

An attraction of GNVQ is that the grading system allows students to make progress during the course. It is understood that students may not reach the standards required until towards the end of the programme. Therefore merits and distinctions are awarded on the basis of the best third of the assembled evidence.

GNVQ Science options

In theory it should be possible for students to tailor GNVQ programmes to match their interests and ambitions but in the early years this is unlikely to happen. At most centres, teachers will make the choice of optional and additional units constrained by timetabling arrangements and the availability of specialist staff. In time, as staff gain confidence in the new award, and develop more resources for supported self-study, we will probably see more choices being made by the students.

The place of GNVQ additional units

A fifteen-unit Advanced GNVQ is equivalent to two A levels. It therefore might occupy about two-thirds of the work for a post-16 student doing a two-year course. Timetable space can be filled in a variety of ways.

- Students can deepen their science education in a particular area by studying **additional** GNVQ Science units. A range of these will be offered by all the awarding bodies. As with optional units, there are no tests for additional units.

- Students can broaden their education within the GNVQ framework by studying extra units (between four and six) drawn from other GNVQ programmes, provided they are drawn from those of the awarding body involved with GNVQ Science at that centre.

- Students can study A or AS level(s). Some schools and colleges believe that universities will look more favourably on GNVQ if students can also show achievement in the traditional university entrance qualification. A common choice here is A or AS level maths, although some centres offer humanities A levels and a few believe that an additional science A level may be appropriate.

- Students can pick up extra GCSEs or take up some more directly career-oriented skills by doing work-related NVQ units.

Teaching and learning GNVQ Science

A new approach

'Take the opportunity to re-think the best way of interesting students in science.'

For many students a GNVQ programme involves a new emphasis in their approach to learning and a new relationship with their teachers. This can be a problem at the start of the course – hence the need for a thorough induction programme (see chapter 5).

Some centres report that girls get off to a much better start than boys. Girls respond well to the relative independence and scope for individual research. They are also likely to more careful and effective in the laboratory.

Lack of confidence and limited mastery of basic science can be a problem in the early stages. Following an initial induction period, many pilot centres have felt the need for a highly structured teaching sequence covering theory and practical skills before their students are ready to attempt assignments requiring planning. In some centres this early phase included whole-class teaching, but students elsewhere were generally working on their own or in groups on tasks of various kinds.

'There is a risk of making the assignments over-elaborate because you are concerned about achieving certain performance criteria. Always remember to look at the assignment from the student's point of view.'

Staff at a college piloting the first round of Intermediate GNVQs in 1992–3 found that assignments based on whole units broken down into smaller tasks worked best. Towards the end of a unit they asked students to design their own 'final' assignment to complete coverage of performance criteria and range. Work on the 'final' assignment helped students to get an overview of the unit and to demonstrate the higher-order planning and data-handling skills which can lead to a merit or distinction classification.

Staff planning a teaching programme aim to use a variety of teaching and learning methods including: lectures, tutorials, discussion, presentations, practical work in the laboratory and in the field, videos and IT sessions, as well as supported self-study and drop-in workshops.

GNVQ assignments

'Allow students plenty of time to draw up action plans. This helps them to see their way through assignments.'

It is difficult to generalize about the relationship between assignments and the specification because different units and elements of GNVQ Science vary markedly. Sometimes it is possible to cover a whole unit in one major assignment. Often a unit has three elements, each of which can be the basis of a single assignment. The pilot version of Intermediate unit 4, however, has three main strands running through the elements and so some pilot centres have devised three assignments, each of which covers performance criteria in the three elements and which between them cover the whole range.

RANGE

The meaning of the term 'assignment' varies from centre to centre. One lecturer or teacher might present a collection of tasks and activities as one big assignment whereas another person might offer the same programme as a series of six to eight separate assignments.

Covering the range

The evidence indicators allow students to sample the range for the topics they will study in depth. Nevertheless portfolios must show that students have covered the full range and, in the mandatory units, basic knowledge of all the range is required for the tests.

The pilot versions of the units have extensive ranges so that coverage has proved difficult. Colleges and schools have used a variety of techniques to overcome the problem. Methods include: keynote lessons by teachers, short tasks focused on particular range dimensions, structured practical work, group discussion and oral questioning.

Staff at a school in the Midlands have devised a series of study guides with questions and short tasks which give students a structure which helps them to cover the range.

Core skills

Most science staff running GNVQ courses like to see core skills integrated with science but they recognize that students need specialist support. Timetabled sessions in maths and IT are common. Science teachers tend to be more confident that they can help students to develop communication skills with little or no extra help.

Amongst science staff there is general dislike for the idea, strongly advocated in some colleges, that there should be a cross-college approach to the teaching of core skills to all students on GNVQ courses.

Students quickly become familiar with the need to find information for themselves by gathering material from several sources. Nevertheless, hunting for appropriate sources in the library and making effective use of them can be a problem. In the early stages it is helpful to set up a 'mini-library' of books and other sources of information in a 'resources box' which goes round with the students to their laboratories and classrooms.

Some centres have found that it is a great help if scientists in the course team have expertise in some of the core skills. At one college the chemist is an IT expert and the physicist a former maths teacher. Nevertheless, as a group this team strongly advocates specialist support for core skills.

Application of number and other aspects of mathematics

The links between GNVQ Science and mathematics involve:

- **core skills** – mastery of 'application of number' at the minimum level required for GNVQ certification

- **maths for science** – the mathematical competence which students need to cope with the GNVQ Science units (which may or may not be achieved by aiming for higher levels of 'application of number' – say level 5 for students on an Advanced science course), and

- **'additionality'** – the extra mathematical competence which students may need if they are to go on to employment or higher education, where they may be expected to be familiar with at least some of the applied mathematics or statistics which features in A level syllabuses.

Our discussions with science and maths teachers show that there can be mutual incomprehension. On the one hand, maths teachers looking at the GNVQ specification cannot easily identify the mathematical implications of the performance criteria and range. On the other hand, science teachers, though they may be able to recognize the mathematical techniques, cannot understand the problems students may have with these techniques. Furthermore science teachers may add to the difficulties by adopting procedures which are 'out-of-date' in terms of modern approaches to maths teaching.

For GNVQ Science, some mathematicians have decided to approach core skills in the spirit of this quotation: 'The time to learn something is when you can't proceed without knowing it.' They think that maths teaching in GNVQ science should respond to need. This means that maths teachers working with GNVQ students have to be willing to take a fresh look at their approach to topics. They may have to set aside the conventional, step-by-step build up from simpler ideas to techniques traditionally perceived as complex. Instead, they may have to plunge in with a 'difficult' technique which students need and then, having demonstrated its value, work back to the more elementary stages underlying the application.

The 'need' provides the motivation. Once students understand the power and value of what they are learning, they are more willing to work through the necessary practice exercises which are generally essential if they are to gain confidence and mastery.

It is not, however, only the maths teachers who have to reconsider their approach. Science teachers have to check their assumptions too. Why the obsession with 'rearranging formulae', for example? How important is this? To what extent does new technology call for a different approach now that programmable and graphics calculators are becoming affordable (in many if not all centres)?

Of course, there are still problems for the maths teacher trying to run tutorials, workshops or supported self-study sessions on a 'need to know' basis. The 'needs' may be very uneven so that the 'load' needs managing and the abilities of the group are likely to be very diverse.

The strategy has to be highly differentiated. This does not necessarily mean that all the teaching has to be based on students working in isolation on a long series of tasks. Solitary toil over worksheets can be a depressing business. There are, fortunately, topics which lend themselves to mixed group-work with 'differentiation by outcome'. As a project we will try to build diversity into any resources we devise to encourage variety and counteract monotony. We do not want students to feel that maths is something you have to suffer alone and in silence.

Links with IT can help. There is a place for whole-group teaching to introduce new techniques with software, the use of graphics calculators and techniques for solving equations graphically. Thereafter students will vary in the speed with which they master the new skills and the extent to which they exploit them for applications of number. Some will be able to tackle much more challenging problems than others.

Application-of-number teaching should not just be a series of routine exercises. Students can be given opportunities for more investigative approaches. Vocational assignments, as well as practice exercises, should give students the chance to learn new mathematical skills and to reflect on their mathematical knowledge.

Information technology

'Take every opportunity to integrate IT into the programme.'

Early access to computers with training in the use of word processing and spreadsheet software can bring a boost to confidence as students experience success and start to produce attractive reports illustrated with charts and diagrams.

This case study describes how one college, with considerable experience of running vocational courses, has applied IT in GNVQ Science.

CASE STUDY

IT FOR GNVQ SCIENCE AT A MIDLANDS COLLEGE

Our system is designed to be embedded in the work of the specialist units, particularly in carrying out assignments where IT is intended to enhance the quality of both the investigation and presentation of the project. It works in the following sequence.

Acquiring skills (tooling up)

We have designed and developed a range of specific manuals from which students acquire the basic skills involved in using a range of applications packages. We have set up a series of tasks which provide the student with a number of opportunities to learn and display proficiency in the various elements. The printouts obtained on completing the tasks are available as evidence of competence in these skills.

Application

At an early point in the academic session specialist lecturers identify the assignments which require IT. We then consult to arrive at a suitable assignment brief which states clearly what is expected of the student and explains how they are to apply IT. The students can then use scheduled IT sessions to carry out the work. We suspend the 'tooling up' process while students are applying IT to a science assignment and then start it up again when the assignment is completed. We have to make sure that the necessary skills and packages have been covered before students start on a science assignment.

Assessment

In the previous BTEC courses, students were graded on each skill area according to their observed performance and the quality of the work they handed in. This work was assessed by both the subject specialist and IT staff. The overall grade was based on their mastery of the basic skills and their ability to utilize and exploit IT to enhance the quality of their work in science.

We intend to continue with this method in principle and to develop the assessment system to cover the new core skills tracking and recording requirements. Most of the elements and criteria are covered in our existing training materials and the work done there can be used as evidence of achieving performance criteria. Work done in science assignments will offer opportunities to display competence in the criteria at merit or distinction level.

Accreditation of prior learning

We intend to use our record sheets to accredit prior learning for students who have already acquired these skills in previous courses. We will expect them to demonstrate the skills in diagnostic tasks. We will encourage students who start with a good level of competence in IT to acquire further skills at a higher level. This we hope will prepare them for the more sophisticated investigative methods used in employment and higher education.

Links with people who use science in their work

Existing contacts and work-experience schemes make good starting points for building links between GNVQ Science and local employers. In some areas the careers service has been helpful in providing information about likely contacts. Often personal contacts and chance encounters have led to successful collaboration. One college in the South east, for example, found that they could base an Advanced assignment around a problem faced by a local canal company with pondweed growth. Another assignment at the same college will produce a report for the local Red Cross training officer.

Local employers or universities can be very helpful when it comes to gaining access to advanced instruments such as spectrometers.

Here are two case studies showing how links can be built between your GNVQ Science course and local industry, commerce and public services. Both case studies include practical advice based on several years experience.

The first case study describes the industry links at a well-established BTEC Science centre. Over the last couple of years the college has found the traditional placements in local industry harder to come by. The staff have taken the opportunity of the new GNVQ programme to engage industry again. So far they have been pleasantly surprised by the willingness of industrialists to get involved.

INDUSTRY LINKS AT A MIDLANDS COLLEGE

Central to the vocational nature of the GNVQ Science must be the involvement of industry, which is easier said than done!

We decided to start by exploring what was available locally with links to the topic which our students were working on at the time. We found plenty of opportunities including: fish farms, mushroom growers, an international centre for courgettes and a maggot farm as well as the more conventional public health laboratories. Also on our list were laboratories for research, environmental health monitoring and the water industry. Far from a shortage we soon realized that we could spend all day everyday in a different place. But what response would we get from our local contacts?

At first we were not sure what we really wanted so we decided to give a short update to all our current contacts. We briefed them about our new GNVQ Science courses. We were seeking their continued support and preparing the ground for later visits and links to our programme.

We felt vulnerable about approaching companies, even ones we felt we knew quite well, because we initially lacked details of the GNVQ specification and were feeling our way into our new programmes.

In the end we chose to work with just one company and explore one GNVQ unit with them. We contacted a small Analytical Service business which was set up only a few years ago. The company is doing real science and making money. We already had some of their technicians on day release with us and we trained their senior manager. Two of us, armed with the GNVQ specifications, spent a morning with the two senior managers. We were surprised by how willing they were to help.

The managers wanted our students to visit them early. They would supply data and real problems; they also offered to mentor students on specific projects and they wanted to come in to spend time with us!

So it is amazingly easy! The difficult part has been finding the development time to build on this. We have been unable to do much more than make a few visits so far. But changes to timetables, a feeling that we have cracked the systems needed and a clear desire to do more, mean we shall be getting to grips with industry very shortly.

Just in case that sounds as if we have been postponing things, here are a few of the industry activities undertaken in the first term of our GNVQ courses.

- A week trip to Paris for a group engaged in assignment work on the Health Service.
- Setting up of science placements in French labs for Easter.
- A meeting with the link engineer who is putting us in touch with several local firms who provide expertise in the technical science area.
- Contact with the Chemical Industrial Association to explore the possibility of a video and presentation for centres to use in GNVQ induction.

■ Seminars on environmental monitoring and auditing for a group of local businesses.

In conclusion, here is some advice based on strategies which have worked for us.

1 Have a good look at the range of possibilities, you'll be surprised – we were.

2 Start small and put in a lot of personal commitment. We do not tend to rely on the careers service or college co-ordinators to make our links, though we know that many careers services do help to arrange placements.

3 Get people in to talk to your students – but structure it carefully.

4 Go to see local concerns at times which suit them and prepare well – expect success.

5 Use your 'link engineer' network – we've been delighted with ours.

6 Be hopeful because companies seem surprisingly willing to help with both materials and staff time – so try to build them into your work and report on its value – some companies may even give you money.

7 Contact the people who can get things done, it can be very frustrating spending time with the wrong individual.

8 Train your students for industry placements and visits because their attitude and behaviour can strengthen or destroy your links.

9 Beware if a company seems to be getting too ambitious about links – try to get them to think small and remember the performance criteria and ranges.

10 Make time to get the link right – that means quite large chunks of time and not for just one person.

11 Realize it takes time to develop the links so be prepared to cultivate them!

The next case study describes a college which has a tradition of inviting speakers into college to talk to the A level science students. Based on this experience the course team decided to ask some of the speakers to talk to the Advanced GNVQ Science students. They hoped that this would not only interest the students but also help them to build evidence for their portfolios.

THE CONTRIBUTION OF VISITING SPEAKERS TO THE GNVQ PROGRAMME AT A COLLEGE IN THE NORTH WEST

One of the advantages of the GNVQ course is that it can allow time for (and credit) visits by students to meet scientists working in local industry. This causes two problems. Firstly it is time consuming and secondly only feasible for a small group of students. Hence the benefit of bringing a speaker into college. This allows a large number of students to benefit from the experience at the same time.

Finding interesting speakers can be a problem and you never know quite how 'good' someone will be until they arrive and talk. Some of the large, recently privatized industries such as electricity, gas and water are good sources of visitors. You must check that the person coming to speak is a scientist and not someone from the PR department.

Local councils employ people who use science in their work, including environmental health officers, who usually make interesting speakers with special relevance to local issues. Whilst most of our speakers come from large organizations, we also find it worthwhile to approach individuals, for example doctors, vets, and others. Our students can sometimes put us in touch with stimulating contributors through their families or friends.

In the past some of our most interesting speakers have come from pressure groups and voluntary organizations. Try getting a speaker in from Greenpeace or Friends of the Earth the week after the representative from British Nuclear Fuels. This usually generates lively debate.

In order to ensure that the talk goes as well as possible we aim for the following format.

1 Discuss in advance with the visiting speaker the nature of the talk. Include in the briefing a little on the background of the students, the level of work and the type of questions that need answering.

2 Keep the talk short. Thirty to forty minutes is usually plenty.

3 Start the talk off with the speaker giving some information about themselves. What sort of qualifications do they have? What sort of industries have they worked in? What is their role in the company?

4 The talk itself. Either an outline of a typical day's work or a case study to show the methods of working out a scientific problem. One of the interesting points that often emerges here is how much time scientists spend not doing science. Large parts of the working day are engaged in report writing, meetings, legal aspects and communicating with others. For instance, a scientist from the National Rivers Authority explained that he spent a lot of time trying to persuade farmers to ensure that their silage clamps did not leak toxic liquor into local rivers.

5 Allow plenty of time for questions. These may arise during the talk, but a section at the end specifically for these is a good idea. There should be no shortage of questions. I do however 'sow the seeds' of questions in the minds of the students during the briefing sessions the week before.

CASE STUDY

▼ *continued from page 26*

6 Ask students to produce written reports on the talk. This will help to reinforce what has been said and provide a lasting record that may be of use in their portfolios.

Two final points. Try to plan speakers as far in advance as possible. This will help you to integrate them with the teaching programme. Secondly do use the visit to 'show off' your college or school, after all many teachers and students visit local industries but only occasionally do representatives from industry come to look at education. We take some time to show visitors around and explain the courses that we offer. This gives us a chance to promote GNVQ Science. At the beginning of the financial year we even have enough money to provide them with a cup of coffee and a plate of sandwiches.

Four case studies

We end this chapter with four case studies from two colleges and two schools to give you some insight into the various ways in which centres are developing their GNVQ programmes. There is a lot of detail which may be helpful if you are thinking about course planning. If you are just looking for a general overview of GNVQ you may prefer to move on to the next chapter.

The first case study describes a well established BTEC centre which decided to transfer from BTEC National Diploma to GNVQ from the start. Relatively generous staffing levels have helped to get the new course off to a good start.

CASE STUDY

GNVQ SCIENCE AT A COLLEGE IN THE MIDLANDS

Staffing

The whole GNVQ Science team is nine staff, four of whom contribute to both the Intermediate as well as the Advanced programme. All have experience of science in industry and experience of teaching vocational courses. For our advanced team we have on the permanent staff both a former MLSO and someone who has practised as a pharmacist.

Our staff are multi-skilled: the physicist has an extremely strong chemistry background and the biologist is at home with chemistry, given her industrial experience. Our technicians have sound industrial experience too and it shows in their ability to contribute to our development work.

▼
▼

Resources

We decided to convert from our BTEC Science programmes to the new GNVQ courses at both Intermediate and Advanced levels in one go. We were committed to doing the same for our Health and social care programme. This meant that hardly anyone in the science school was left out of GNVQ developments. So much so that staff complain that there is too much talk about GNVQ in the staff room.

At the moment we enjoy a relatively generous 'unit of resource'. Across the college we can allocate 22 hours per week for the 36 weeks of a full-time programme. The staffing level is planned to cover this and allows a budget for part-timers too.

We do not expect to be able to maintain such a high level of resource, so we decided to deploy as much staff time as possible in the first GNVQ year to allow us to get to grips with the qualification without compromising the high quality which moderators have come to expect from us.

What does all that mean in terms of programme?

The level of staffing means that in the first year we can aim to complete the mandatory Advanced units with an allocation of 54 hours per unit.

Our whole GNVQ team explored various approaches to timetabling the Advanced programme at one of our regular workshop sessions. We allocated units to small groups of staff who looked in more detail at the specifications. They reported back a week later and we were able to assign units to staff based on their wishes, expertise and experience. We next mapped a programme for the year with a more or less logical sequence for the Advanced units. We took advice from colleagues who had piloted Health and social care. They strongly recommended that we should work on a unit-by-unit basis.

A smaller team organized the programme for the one-year Intermediate course. We were able to allocate 72 hours per unit. The pilot units are clearly composed of biology, chemistry and physics sections so we chopped the units up and allocated them to three specialist teachers.

We have an interesting contrast of working unit-by-unit in the Advanced course while picking out biology, chemistry and physics strands at Intermediate level. We think both systems will work.

We cover core skills ourselves and do not have to go outside the science school for input. Our ability to deliver the whole programme within the team is very important to us. We own it and we are responsible for its quality. We are, however, not so sure that we can undertake the remedial number work which some of our Intermediate students need.

CASE STUDY

▼ *continued from page 28*

Tutoring

We chose tutors with experience of action planning and building a portfolio of evidence. One of the tutors has been deeply involved in vocational science in Youth Training. Another has experience of building up our science-industry contacts and can also handle the IT needed to produce the course documentation we are inventing.

Thanks to the relatively generous staffing this year we have been able to timetable course-team sessions free of teaching so that we can collaborate to develop the new programmes. During the first term we decided to double the number of tutors and the time allocated to tutorial sessions in the light of experience. We already have staff trained as internal verifiers so we are using them to guide the design of our systems.

A feature of this next case study is the way in which the course team collaborates on a unit by unit approach to the GNVQ. Note too the commitment to setting assignments in vocational contexts.

CASE STUDY

GNVQ SCIENCE AT A COLLEGE IN THE NORTH EAST

We are offering GNVQ Science at both Advanced and Intermediate levels but here we will concentrate on our Advanced course.

Staffing

We run a block timetable with 15 hours contact time per week for the basic Advanced GNVQ. Students may study additional courses in other blocks. In the first year the staffing of our Advanced course is as follows. A block corresponds to 6×50 minute sessions:

- biologist (half a block)
- chemist (half a block)
- physicist who also covers IT (1 block)
- mathematician (half a block)
- English teacher (half a block).

In the second year of the course we have decided to allocate a full block to each of the science specialists who will then also be responsible for core skills.

We have a timetabled, weekly meeting for all members of the course team. In addition the team leader has one free lesson for administration. The regular team meeting is absolutely essential for the careful planning we need for our unit-by-unit approach. All staff, including core-skill teachers, are training as assessors and we have one specialist internal verifier. We think that the internal verifier also needs timetable remission to cope with all the requirements of the role.

Programme planning

The course team decided that we would provide the best education for the students on our Advanced programme by concentrating on one unit at a time while integrating pilot unit 8 and core skills. This approach provides continuity for the students and means that they can prepare for tests one at a time. The disadvantage is that not all staff are familiar with the equipment, techniques and theory related to the unit. Also, because of timetabling restrictions, students have to move rooms between sessions even though they continue to work on the same topic. Students are happy with this approach.

Sometimes core-skill staff supervise students while they are doing their science. At other times they make a specialist input related to students' needs for their next assignment.

Autumn term

Weeks 1 and 2: Induction, industrial visits, diagnostic testing and a team-building day

Weeks 3 and 4: A study of health and safety in parallel with basic teaching on core skills

Weeks 5 to 11: Pilot unit 7 divided into two: with half the time covering ecosystems and the rest of the time studying the living body

Weeks 12 and 13 Pilot unit 5 starting with a series of tasks which will allow students to practise the skills they will need for assignments to achieve 5.1

We will spend the first four or five weeks in the spring term completing unit 5 and then move on to unit 4. Overall we hope to cover 5 units in the first year integrated with most of a sixth unit (unit 8) and the core skills.

Approaches to teaching and learning

Working unit-by-unit means that we have to be well organized. A subject specialist takes on the role of 'unit leader' and is responsible for planning the approach to the unit and preparing the student materials. We aim to prepare drafts at least 2 weeks in advance to allow time for a review of the opportunities to develop core skills and to help other staff to identify the contributions they can make to the programme.

Students learn most of their science from the programme of tasks and assignments. This is backed up with two to three hours per week of formal teaching. Teaching methods used include lectures, computer programmes and videos. We set our assignments in context. In unit 7, for example, students studied ecology from the perspective of a scientist working in the field and the 'living body' from the point of view of a doctor or sports specialist working with people.

▼
▼

Our assignments consist of a number of discrete activities. Early in the course these are often quite prescriptive but are becoming more open-ended as the course progresses. Sometimes we find it appropriate to cover a unit in three assignments (one per element). Sometimes, however, it will be more appropriate to have one assignment for a unit to allow more scope for planning by the students.

Tutoring

Each student has a GNVQ tutor who takes responsibility for counselling and action planning. This includes arrangements for work experience. Tutorials take place during normal contact time or outside timetabled sessions at the convenience of the tutor and tutee. We will consider instead special tutorial time next year.

Science at work

Our programme includes two to three weeks of work experience in year 2 for Advanced students. We have links with local employers which allow us to make visits to manufacturing industry, a leisure centre and a botanical centre. We invite visiting speakers to talk to our students and take advantage of the Neighbourhood Engineers scheme. We encourage students to collect and process data from industrial organizations.

Problems

Perhaps our biggest problem is to get students to keep to deadlines. After seven weeks on an Advanced unit only one student had completed all the work, many others had almost finished, but a few had completed very little.

Running a course of this kind requires staff to be well organized, to follow instructions from other staff clearly and be willing to alter their roles in the classroom. Management support in terms of room allocations, free time and timetable is also important. We have made a good start with respect to these issues but still have a few problems to resolve.

GNVQ Intermediate

We have given our Intermediate programme a strong 'sports' flavour. In addition to the main science programme our students can take on additional elements: the Sports Leaders award and GNVQ Leisure and tourism unit 2 (Organizing an event). Within the science programme we will offer 'Sports science' as one of the optional units. As well as the subject specialists we have included a PE teacher in the course team who is also responsible for communication skills. The physicist covers IT and we have a mathematician for the application of number.

As at Advanced level, students work on one unit at a time starting with unit 2. We are integrating unit 1 with the other units. Our second optional unit will be Earth science because the chemist on the team is also a geologist.

We find that we can cover much of the range in Intermediate units through practical activities but in some units it is so wide that students have to work from secondary sources to cover the ground.

The course team at the school described in the next case study used industry links when planning their GNVQ programmes. The teaching modules cut across GNVQ units and are developed in the context of local opportunities for science-based employment.

GNVQ SCIENCE AT A SCHOOL IN THE WEST MIDLANDS

Timetabling and staffing

Both our Intermediate and Advanced students are timetabled for sixteen periods per week in the laboratory with the support of science staff. This works out at 9 hours 20 minutes per week – the same amount of contact time that a two A level student would have. In addition our GNVQ students have four periods timetabled with the mathematician in our team and another four periods with a member of our English department who helps them with communication skills. In common with all post-16 students at the school their programme also contains two periods of extension studies and two periods of PE/Games. This gives them a total of 28 out of 40 timetabled periods of contact time per week (16 hours 20 minutes). The remaining twelve periods are self-study time, although some of the students are doing other courses in addition to GNVQ Science.

The programme is staffed by a team of six science teachers, a mathematician and an English specialist who is also form tutor to the nineteen Intermediate students who have started the course. The science staff cover a range of specialisms – chemistry, physics, biology and geology. Four out of the sixteen periods of laboratory time are staffed with a pair of staff working together – the other periods have just one teacher with the students.

The Intermediate and Advanced level students are timetabled at the same time, although two laboratories are available and they tend to split into separate groups. There have been times when we have felt stretched with just one member of staff supporting both groups (a total of 30 students when they are all present) even though we have developed a supported self-study style. Next year we will try to staff the course with a team of three teachers for all 16 periods in order to cope with the expected demands of Intermediate students as well as first and second year Advanced groups. However, this may prove to be too expensive on staffing and we may be forced to compromise.

Induction

Our induction module lasted for three weeks and was based on the theme of 'What do scientists do?' We linked up with a local dairy to provide the context for a couple of practical assignments. All students made a visit to the dairy. Both Intermediate and Advanced level groups worked together on the same induction assignments although there were some differentiated tasks. On the whole it went well and comments from students were generally positive but some of the practical work needs refining. We hope to make more of the accreditation of prior learning (APL) next year.

continued from page 32

CASE STUDY

Programme planning

Our programme is integrated and based on a series of 'teaching' modules. All of the planned modules cover elements from at least two different units. However, we have not yet considered the optional units and it could be that these are delivered as separate units towards the end of the course.

It's difficult to say how much time is being devoted to a unit because of our integrated approach but our modules are about 6 weeks long. We are unlikely to offer students a choice of optional units. The major constraint is the lack of time available to prepare assignments and other materials. We will, however, be working towards offering a choice in the future.

Core skills

The maths and English specialists in our team are responsible for supporting students with core skills and assessing the application of number and communication units. We would have liked an IT expert on the team but this proved impossible to staff. The help of these team members is proving to be extremely valuable.

Teaching and learning styles

The whole of the programme is being delivered through assignments. These vary in length although the longer ones tend to be split up into a number of tasks. Intermediate level assignments tend to be shorter than those given to Advanced students.

The next case study describes a school which has developed strategies for running GNVQ courses with limited contact time. Student numbers are small in the first year so Advanced and Intermediate groups work together.

CASE STUDY

GNVQ SCIENCE IN AN 11–18 RURAL COMPREHENSIVE SCHOOL IN THE NORTH WEST

The school is voluntary controlled and co-educational in a small market town with a large rural catchment. There are approximately 930 students of whom 130 are in the sixth form. During the pilot year we offered GNVQ Science at both Intermediate and Advanced levels. At the same time our sixth form curriculum included two other GNVQs at both levels, eighteen A and AS levels and three GCSEs. How did we 'squeeze a quart into a pint pot' and still offer what we believe to be a high-quality GNVQ course?

The following factors are all relevant.

Grouping

The six Advanced and three Intermediate students are in a single group. The nature of our course, and delivery styles employed, mean that this has not been a problem.

▼
▼

Contact time

We allocate 5 hours 50 minutes (5 x 70 minute periods) to the GNVQ Science course with science specialists. In addition students have access to a flexible period of 2 hours 20 minutes (2 x 70 minute periods) with the school-industry co-ordinator. This time is shared with GNVQ students in other vocational areas. Students also have a further 2 hours 20 minutes of 'designated study time' during which they work unsupervised on tasks agreed with GNVQ staff during weekly action planning meetings. Most Advanced level students also study an A or AS level in addition to the general programme while Intermediate students take English and/or maths GCSE in addition to the general programme.

Figure 3.1
Some typical timetables

NAME: <u>AN INTERMEDIATE LEVEL GNVQ STUDENT</u>
FORM: _____

	p1	p2	p3	p4	p5	p6	p7	p8
Monday	FREE		GNVQ Science		GNVQ Science		GCSE English lang.	
Tuesday	Tutor period (general programme)		Young enterprise (general programme)		GCSE maths		Designated GNVQ study time	
Wednesday	GNVQ Science		GNVQ support		General programme		Games	
Thursday	Designated GNVQ study time		GCSE English lang.		General programme		FREE	
Friday	GCSE maths		GNVQ Science		GNVQ Science		FREE	

NAME: <u>AN ADVANCED LEVEL GNVQ STUDENT</u>
FORM: _____

	p1	p2	p3	p4	p5	p6	p7	p8
Monday	A level		GNVQ Science		GNVQ Science		FREE	
Tuesday	Tutor period (general programme)		A level		Designated GNVQ study time		FREE	
Wednesday	GNVQ Science		GNVQ support		Young enterprise (general programme)		Games	
Thursday	A level		GNVQ support		General programme		FREE	
Friday	Designated GNVQ study time		GNVQ Science		GNVQ Science		A level	

Teaching methods

With Intermediate and Advanced students in the same group, and with a relatively small amount of contact time, we have to rely on a very student-centred, flexible approach.

1 Assignments are introduced to relevant groups of students (Intermediate or Advanced). Students are given an assignment brief and relevant part of specifications.

2 Supported self-study to provide background, and cover some of range. This involves some didactic input and 'expert' input via visits or guest speakers.

3 Each student carefully prepares an action plan for the assignment. This is discussed with the tutor and may be modified several times before tutor and student agree. The plan has to show which aspects of the core skills will be covered.

4 Weekly individual action planning takes place with student and tutor agreeing tasks and deadlines, and evaluating the previous week's work.

5 The assignment is completed by a rigid deadline.

6 Assignment evaluation occurs with the whole group along with any necessary additional input, to ensure full range cover.

7 Assignments are assessed and evaluated with the student.

8 Summative records are completed and, if all evidence for unit is complete, and range is fully covered, the relevant unit test is ordered.

Attitude of senior management team

Our senior staff are fully committed to GNVQ. The programme of GCSEs traditionally offered to students intending to leave at the end of year 12, has already been replaced with Intermediate GNVQ (with the exception of English and maths), and our sixth form curriculum is basically A/AS levels, and GNVQ. To a small extent other courses are 'subsidizing' GNVQ but we see this as a long-term investment.

The nature of the school

In the compact community of the school sixth form, the centre co-ordinator and programme co-ordinator see students every day. 'Ad-hoc' action planning tutorials frequently take place in the corridor when students and tutors are passing. The GNVQ staff are based next to rooms in which GNVQ students work, and, while more formal contact time is desirable, the good will and flexibility of staff involved still, we believe, allows us to offer a high-quality course.

Personnel

We think that it would be a major error to force a member of staff to become involved in GNVQ if they are not committed to the course. Staff need appropriate support, induction and INSET to give them the confidence necessary to tackle a very new way of teaching and assessing. All staff involved have either passed the TDLB assessor awards (units D32 and D33) or are currently being trained. The centre co-ordinator, who is also programme co-ordinator for science, has passed the internal verifiers award (unit D34). Staff involved in a GNVQ Science programme have to work hard but are rewarded by enthusiastic, committed students who take pride in producing high quality work. We have been fortunate in having staff who are 'GNVQ converts'.

At the time of writing all students on the course are enjoying the work and have no regrets about choosing GNVQ Science. Some of the work produced has been of a particularly pleasing standard. Our approach certainly puts pressure on students. They have to make effective and consistent use of all their time to complete assignments on schedule. As you might expect, some find this tricky.

4

Staffing and timetabling GNVQ Science

Management issues

Initiating a GNVQ programme can be a creative process but it is inevitably hard work for all concerned.

Early experience from colleges and schools suggests that whole-hearted support from senior management is crucial as staff build a course team, make plans, assemble resources and put in place all the requirements for a successful programme.

'Make sure you get backing from senior management. Impress on them the amount of extra time and training needed by GNVQ staff.'

To highlight some of the implications of involvement with GNVQs we start this chapter with a case study from a large college to show that introducing GNVQ has big implications for the management of a college or school. This college is introducing GNVQ Science in September 1994.

CASE STUDY

INTRODUCING GNVQS AT A COLLEGE IN THE NORTH EAST

We see the introduction of GNVQs as an opportunity to implement a number of major changes so that we can offer a more client-centred curriculum with greater flexibility.

Senior management has made two important decisions:

■ to switch to GNVQs as soon as they are generally available

■ to go with one awarding body as far as possible.

We have chosen BTEC for Advanced and Intermediate GNVQs because many areas of the college are already familiar with their qualifications, as are the higher education establishments to which we commonly send students.

The early commitment to GNVQs from our management team has been central to their successful introduction. Although it has meant that changes needed for the new programmes have all had to happen together, staff have been able to understand the rationale for the changes and to know in advance the timetable for change.

Figure 4.1 shows several cross-college initiatives in response to the decision to move to GNVQs.

▼
▼

▼ *continued from page 36*

CASE STUDY

Figure 4.1

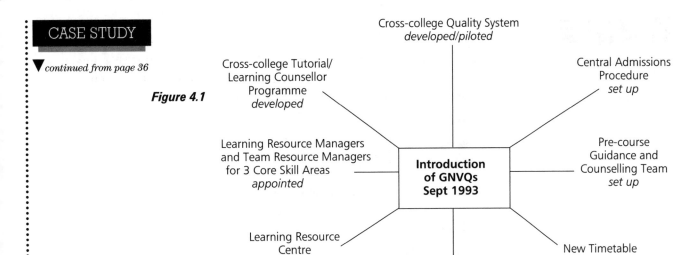

Cross-college Quality System
developed/piloted

Cross-college Tutorial/
Learning Counsellor
Programme
developed

Central Admissions
Procedure
set up

Learning Resource Managers
and Team Resource Managers
for 3 Core Skill Areas
appointed

**Introduction
of GNVQs
Sept 1993**

Pre-course
Guidance and
Counselling Team
set up

Learning Resource
Centre
set up

New Timetable
introduced

Curriculum Co-ordinators
in place at levels 2 and 3

Timetabling

The college is the only major FE provider in the region. We serve a large rural community and we have been teaching our A level and GCSE curriculum on subject days to minimize travelling time and costs for part-time students. Since staff prefer this system we have decided to retain subject days in a new timetable. Each GNVQ team plans their programme with 12 class contact hours over two full days of the week.

We set a basic block system of the timetable. Timetablers from all areas of the college then meet to liaise and 'bargain' to ensure that likely combinations of GNVQ with GCSEs, A levels, NVQs and other courses are possible. This really puts our communication skills to the test!

The system offers a great variety of individual programmes to students (see figure 4.2).

Figure 4.2
A sample of GNVQ timetables

Advanced GNVQ in Leisure and tourism

Monday	GNVQ Day		
Tuesday	Free Time	Coaching Award Programme	
Wednesday	Private Study Day		Tutorial
Thursday	GNVQ Day		
Friday	'A' Level P.E.		

Intermediate GNVQ in Leisure and tourism

Monday	GNVQ Day		
Tuesday	Uniformed Services Course Career Preparation	Uniformed Services Course Coaching Awards	
Wednesday	GCSE P.E.		Tutorial
Thursday	GNVQ Day		
Friday	Private Study Day		

Intermediate GNVQ Health and social care

Monday	GCSE English		Tutorial
Tuesday	GNVQ Day		
Wednesday	Study Time	Free Time	
Thursday	GNVQ Day		
Friday	Placement		

▼ *continued from page 37*

With the introduction of more GNVQs in September 1994 this timetabling will become increasingly complex. We are thinking of offering our science programmes with a 'flavour' and are currently discussing options such as:

- Science with Business
- Science with Health studies
- Science with Sports studies
- Science with Environmental studies.

Admissions

Now that we have changed from traditional courses to individualized student programmes, we have developed a central admissions procedure through the college advice centre. This helps us to keep track of the students as they progress through the college and beyond. The system also allows us to record the information needed by the Further Education Funding Council (FEFC) for funding purposes.

To meet the increased need for accurate advice we have set up a central pre-course counselling and guidance team of eleven people, one from each programme area. These people are our 'experts'. We expect them to talk to any prospective student and give informed advice, so that course teams do not have to get involved.

We are now piloting this system. Clearly its success depends on the quality of the information given to the guidance team by course-team leaders, careers advisers, timetablers, and higher education co-ordinators. Once briefed, members of the central team will be able to guide individual students on a route appropriate to their qualifications on entry and their chosen career.

Tutorial support

We have recently extended our tutorial programme so that all students with 12 or more hours on their timetable are entitled to an hour a week with a personal tutor. We hope to limit tutor group size to 15 students but this is proving difficult.

In GNVQs the purpose of the tutorial hour has to be more clearly defined. This has prompted us to rename tutors as 'learning counsellors' emphasizing that their major job is to help students develop the skills they need to manage and take control of their own learning.

We are developing a framework which supports staff in the key tasks and activities associated with this new role such as:

- checking that student timetables actually work
- helping students to identify their learning needs
- suggesting ways of meeting those needs
- developing personal and study skills in learners
- discussing problems related to any aspect of student life
- helping students with Records of Achievement

▼ *continued from page 38*

- progression counselling and career guidance, together with
- a host of administrative tasks associated with reporting progress, parents evenings, UCAS forms and so on.

We have produced a resource file to help learning counsellors. The file contains a suggested calendar of events highlighting key dates for administrative and other tasks. The file covers both one-year and two-year programmes. It includes a schedule for review and target-setting sessions with tutees together with sample record sheets. It also includes suggested activities for developing study and personal skills.

Our programme is not meant to be prescriptive or complete and indeed is not without its teething problems. It is a suggested framework which allows flexibility for one-to-one reviewing, small or whole group work; it recognizes that tutorials should be largely student-led. It does, however, offer a starting point which we expect to amend as we develop the role of the learning counsellor.

Learning resource centre

Although the tutorial system helps students identify their learning support needs, we recognize that we have to improve our support services. We are updating and bringing together facilities previously spread throughout the college to establish a large learning resource centre. The learning resource manager and her team are working very closely with the GNVQ course teams.

Core skills

Across the college GNVQ teams adopt different approaches to designing their programme. In art and design there is full integration of units but the business team is working on a unit-by-unit basis. In some programmes, core-skill specialists have been included in the GNVQ teams but in others the lecturers have decided to cover core skills themselves with the help of specialists as consultants. The aim is to ensure full coverage of the range in vocational contexts where possible.

Areas of core skill development which fall outside the planned programme are identified. They are catered for by additional activities either with the course team, in the learning resource centre, or with input from a core-skill specialist.

Staff development and curriculum support

We have curriculum co-ordinators for Intermediate and Advanced programmes across the college. They monitor, support and advise course teams.

Our programme of staff development has included GNVQ awareness-raising events and sessions to explore programme design, core skills and assessment. We also have events to support learning counsellors.

Development time

There are fewer barriers across the path to introducing GNVQs than there have been in some previous vocational courses. In particular there is no requirement for institutional links between the school or college and local industry. Teachers and lecturers do not necessarily need industrial or commercial experience and there is no mandatory work experience for students.

'Arrange to spend time with the staff of a pilot centre – it's the best INSET you will ever get.'

Even so there is much to do because each college or school has to work out an interpretation of the specification which helps students to meet the performance criteria. Centres also have to find ways of assessing and crediting achievements in a manageable way. Our project publications will be a help but they cannot replace the hard task of innovation which falls on each and every course team.

Even centres with experience of running BTEC First and National Diploma courses have much to do as they re-work their courses to fit the new structure of units, elements and performance criteria. They have to rewrite their assignments substantially to match the new criteria.

The GNVQ specification describes outcomes. This means that the specification lacks context which makes it hard to get a sense of what an attractive GNVQ course is like.

This lack of context is, however, one of the potential strengths of the system because it allows course teams to develop teaching and learning programmes which meet the interests and ambitions of their students. There is the opportunity to build links with local people who use science in their work and take advantage of visits, outside speakers and industrial links.

Staff preparing to run a GNVQ need release from some other duties to allow them to plan a high quality programme.

Course-team meetings

'Press hard to get a timetabled course-team meeting and make sure that tutorial time is built in to the programme.'

Staff at some centres began regular team meetings at least a term before their courses began. Subsequently they have had timetabled meetings bringing together tutors, science specialists and core-skills teachers. Those who have experienced this arrangement cannot imagine running their programme successfully without this support.

Others, less fortunate, meet from time to time by arranging team meetings in departmental time or on staff-development days. All too often this means that it is difficult to bring the whole team together.

Listening to discussion among centres, we think it vital that newcomers to GNVQ press hard for regular course-team meetings to plan and monitor the new programme.

Timetabling

A GNVQ Science timetable typically has these components, which may or may not be integrated.

- Science (typically 10–16 hours)
- core skills (typically 2–5 hours)
- tutorial (typically 0.5–2 hours) together, with
- drop-in workshops, GCSE or A/AS courses (very variable).

It is impossible to give precise guidelines about timing because there is great variation in the definition of class contact time. Some schools and colleges supplement normal class periods with workshops, tutorials and sessions in resource or IT centres.

Most centres expect to cover a GNVQ unit in 45–60 hours of contact time with Advanced units nearer the lower end of the range and Intermediate units nearer the upper end. In the early part of the course the pilot centres have often spent much longer than this. One college integrating core skills and pilot unit 8 with all the other Advanced units estimated a total of 80 hours contact time for each of units 1 to 7.

Colleges moving to GNVQ from BTEC courses have generally retained the same total contact time. At Advanced level this allows them to offer a GNVQ qualification with 16 science units which is the pattern familiar to university admissions tutors who have accepted students with BTEC National Diplomas in the past.

Staff in the pilot centres seem to prefer teaching sessions of at least 2 hours. Some have half-day or even whole-day sessions. Longer periods of time give more scope for planning both before and during a practical investigation. They allow students to carry through a complete procedure without an artificial break. There are, however, some schools and colleges running the GNVQ with 1.5 hour timetable sessions or even mainly 40 to 50 minute lessons.

In an ideal world a GNVQ group would have a 'home' room or laboratory. Such a base is a great help when students are involved in a long-running series of assignment tasks which may not fit comfortably into timetabled sessions.

Several pilot centres, like the college featured in the case study on pages 36–39, point out the need to rethink their pastoral tutorial system. The conventional system may not serve the needs of GNVQ students. Tutorial time is so precious that it must be integrated into the GNVQ programme of teaching and learning and not retained as a free-standing element of college or school life.

Programme structure

Generally staffing and timetabling arrangements keep staff working in their own specialisms – but there are exceptions. The table shows some of the ways that pilot centres are planning to cover the Advanced science units in a two-year programme. At Advanced level it has been common, in the pilot year, to run units 1 and 8 across the whole year, integrating them with other units.

Table 4.1

Centre	Year 1 – Advanced	Year 2 – Advanced
A	8 mandatory units – keeping biology, chemistry and physics separate and running three units in parallel	4 optional units and 4 additional units
B	4 mandatory units and 4 optional units – taught in parallel by specialists working largely in their own fields	4 mandatory units with extra optional units or A/AS courses
C	6–8 mandatory units – taught one at a time in series by all teachers co-operating as a science team	The remaining mandatory units plus 4 optional units with additional components from other GNVQ programmes

Running mandatory and optional units together helps to spread out the external tests. Teachers are also finding opportunities to integrate units. Work started in a mandatory unit can be extended and elaborated in a related optional unit.

Some centres with limited contact time realize that it will be difficult to complete 8 units in the first year. They find 6 units to be a more realistic target.

Some staff think that record-keeping, coherence and students' understanding of the course are enhanced by organizing the programme on a unit-by-unit basis. Others believe that vocational relevance is enhanced by devising a series of teaching modules to match opportunities for science-based employment.

Most centres tell us that staff have to choose the optional units, at least in the early years. One school is planning to offer a limited choice of options in their Advanced course by offering three routes: a physics/maths route, a biology/chemistry route and a general route.

One centre is considering the possibility of allowing some students to exploit particular interests by devising their own assignments for optional units. This would give students a chance to choose options and, if it goes well, allow them to show their powers of planning and information gathering.

Some centres with small numbers of students are combining their Advanced and Intermediate students. One or two centres report that this works well (see the case study on pages 33–35) but others are more doubtful. One school points out that the courses are quite separate so that common activities are not appropriate. In any case, students moving on from the Intermediate to the Advanced course will not expect to repeat the same activities.

Additional components

Intermediate

Some schools and colleges have decided to stop running GCSE repeat programmes and to replace them with Intermediate GNVQs. In general, however, they will continue to offer GCSE English and mathematics to GNVQ students who want at least a grade C pass.

Advanced

Pilot centres have strong but contrasting views about the nature and purpose of Advanced additional components. There seem to be three general attitudes.

- The basic GNVQ with 12 science units and 3 core skill units is, and should be, an acceptable preparation for employment or higher education.

- The target should be a GNVQ with 16–18 science units – achieved by covering 4–6 additional units.

- Students should take one AS or A course to supplement the 'double subject' GNVQ.

In the pilot centres, some students on the Advanced course have also been repeating GCSE maths or English if they have not already passed these subjects at grade C or above.

What about the Y-model?

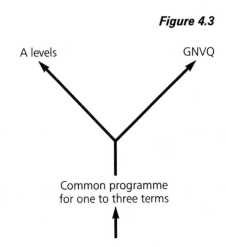

Figure 4.3

Before GNVQ, a few colleges were exploring the Y-model as a means to deferring the choice between an academic or vocational course as long as possible. In this model, all students entering year 12 to study science follow a common programme for one, two or three terms before splitting between the academic (A level) or vocational (GNVQ) route.

An attraction of the Y-model is the apparent opportunity to have larger teaching groups for at least part of a post-16 programme. There are, however, formidable obstacles when it comes to registration, fees, teaching approaches and assessment.

The centres we have worked with are sceptical about the feasibility of the Y-model so long as A level and GNVQ retain their existing characteristics. In most centres the approaches to teaching and learning are very different in the two types of programme. It is also burdensome to require likely A level candidates to start building portfolios of accredited evidence if this is going to be unnecessary once they split off as a group preparing for external examinations.

The next case study describes how a course team prepared to start up Intermediate GNVQ Science in a large FE college. Here you will find an overview of the programme for the whole year complete with a timetable for testing.

GNVQ SCIENCE AT A COLLEGE IN NORTHERN IRELAND

They say August is a wicked month, but in 1993 we knew September would be worse. We were to be a pilot college for GNVQ Intermediate level in science. There are so many questions, so few answers and so little time.

Although some preliminary meetings had been held over the summer, a lot of planning remained to be done. The teaching team were granted a three day residential development session at a local hotel. On the first day we were briefed by consultants from our awarding body. After that, it was up to us!

But the ideas really did flow. Who was it that said nothing concentrates the mind quite like the prospect of imminent hanging?

Our team consisted of three science teachers, three teachers specializing in information technology, application of number, and communication respectively, and a co-ordinator who is also the internal verifier.

Timetabling

When we drew up a timetable for the course, we tried to keep in mind the following needs.

■ Regular team meetings (1 hour per week)

■ formalized review sessions

■ specialist core skills tutors

■ time for directed private study, research, and project work

■ space for additional studies such as GCSE English, and maths.

Our timetable is shown in figure 4.4. A brief summary goes something like this.

Figure 4.4

GNVQ Intermediate Level in Science					
Timetable 1993 – 94					
Subject	Course Div	Day	Room	Time	Hrs
Science	SCI	Mon	D21	0900–1100	2
Science	SCI		C21	1115–1315	2
Research			Lib	1400–1545	1.45
Core Skills	COR	Tue	C21	0900–1040	1.40
Research			Lib	1100–1300	2.0
Review	Tut		C21	1400–1500	1.0
Science	SCI	Wed	D21	0900–1030	1.30
Science	SCI		D4	1115–1315	2
Core Skills	COR	Thur	C26	0900–1040	1.40
Science	SCI		D4	1100–1230	1.30
Science	SCI		C21	1415–1545	1.30
Review	TUT	Fri	D28	0900–0930	0.30
Portfolio			Lib	0930–1100	1.30
Core	COR		C21	1115–1255	1.40

Science: 10 hours 30 minutes per week (3 tutors × 3 hr 30 each)

Core skills: 5 hours per week (3 tutors × 1 hr 40 each)

Reviews: 1 hour 30 minutes per week (3 tutors × 0 hr 30 each)

Directed study/portfolio building: 5 hours 15 minutes per week

Team meeting: 1 hour per week

Space in the timetable means that students have the option of taking selected GCSEs as additional studies.

CASE STUDY

▼ *continued from page 44*

The assessment framework

We recognized that mandatory unit 1 (Working on scientific tasks) would pervade the work in most of the other units and would not have to be delivered separately. Since there are external tests for each of the other three mandatory units, we wanted to spread these out as much as possible.

We were determined that the achievement of core skills would be as fully integrated as possible with the achievement of science skills – this is where our weekly team meetings come in useful.

The elements in the mandatory units fall fairly clearly into either biology, chemistry, or physics activities, and so we divided up the work accordingly. We took the view that parts of BTEC optional unit 5 should be done before parts of unit 2. We also wanted to offer some choice of optional units so we planned to cover three of the four in phase 5.

As it turned out, our assessment plans fell into five overlapping phases.

Phase 1 Induction
13–24 September

Phase 2 Explore materials (unit 2) and Working on scientific tasks (unit1)
27 September–3 December
External test (unit 2) Jan 1994

Phase 3 Making useful products (unit 3) and Working on scientific tasks (unit1)
22 November–21 January
External tests (unit 3) March 1994

Phase 4 Control systems (unit 4) and Working on scientific tasks (unit1)
10 January–25 March
External test (unit 4) May 1994

Phase 5 Nature of everyday changes (BTEC optional unit 5)
Energy and the motor car (BTEC optional unit 6)
Investigating life (BTEC optional unit 7)
11 April–10 June

What are the students like? The next case study describes a group of Advanced students in a large college involved with vocational science for the first time. We are not suggesting that this is a typical group; we know that the first GNVQ Science students are very diverse in their attitudes, abilities, qualifications and expectations. Note that in this college, most students take an A level alongside their GNVQ course.

ADVANCED GNVQ SCIENCE STUDENTS AT A COLLEGE IN THE SOUTH WEST

Entry qualifications

We have a group of fifteen students. Their qualifications range from four to nine GCSEs at grade B or C. Five of the students have at least one grade A among their results. Two of them attempted A levels last year but found the style of the courses too demanding. They are now trying GNVQ Science with one A level.

Science background

Most of the students studied separate sciences at GCSE. Only three followed a dual-award course. All have studied physics with considerable success gaining at least a C grade. The one student to get an E has decided to retake. Five of the students have not studied biology at GCSE and four did not take chemistry.

Programmes of study

Most of our students are taking one A level alongside their GNVQ. The range of A level subjects includes: geography, law, mathematics, psychology and computer studies. Students not taking an A level are retaking GCSEs or following a vocational course in PE or photography.

Aspirations of the students

Five of the students are fairly sure that they do not want to go onto HE. Three have definite plans and hope for jobs with the police force, fire brigade or in photography. The rest of the group hope to take a degree course.

5

Induction

CONSOLIDATE PRIOR
KNOWLEDGE
ASSESS OWN PERFORMANCE

ACCREDITATION

*'Try not to overwhelm students
with too much GNVQ jargon –
introduce it gradually.'*

*'Students needed the time to make
mistakes and get a feel for the
GNVQ style of working.'*

The over-riding objective of the first few weeks of a GNVQ course is to set
students on the way to becoming autonomous, reflective learners with a
strong sense of responsibility and ownership for what they do. Sixteen
year-olds with a background of National Curriculum GCSEs may have to
adapt to the culture of GNVQ and to the notion of building up a portfolio of
evidence to demonstrate that they have met the performance criteria of all
the elements.

Student attitudes to induction

When they start their post-16 course, students want to feel that they are
making progress straight away on a well-planned and purposeful
programme. Students may find the term 'induction' offputting because
they think they are wasting time. In response you can plan an opening unit
of work which starts all sorts of induction processes but without using the
term. Induction does not stop suddenly at the end of this opening part of
the programme; it goes on throughout the GNVQ course as students
progressively become – we all hope – autonomous, competent and
confident practitioners in the world of science.

Students come to school or college to study and learn. They want to be
busy from the start. They also seem to appreciate a strong vocational focus
early on.

Students often have prejudices about what counts as 'work'. Building up a
set of notes, for example, gives students a sense of progress even if they do
not know or understand them. GNVQ induction has to encourage students
and give them a sense of achievement and success straight away. It may be
that they can begin to produce evidence which meets performance criteria
in core skills right from the start.

Bear in mind that many students lack confidence at the beginning of a
GNVQ programme. They may need boosting after a relatively poor
performance at GCSE. They may feel that they have 'failed' to get onto a A
level course. Effective induction can help to build confidence and not
reinforce feelings of failure.

Length of the induction programme

Induction programmes vary from a few days to eight weeks, with most
centres operating a one or two week programme. Some induction
programmes are organized on a faculty or college-wide basis and are
often used as diagnostic periods to settle students into different levels of
GNVQ, or even to decide whether they should follow a vocational or
academic route.

Those with experience of 'supported self-study' at A level stress how important it is to develop the right 'culture' and that the process cannot be hurried. This suggests the need for something longer rather than shorter. GNVQ programmes rely heavily on student-centred learning. If this is to work students must develop learning skills for themselves and encounter a wide range of teaching and learning strategies at the beginning of the course.

The length of an induction programme is partly a matter of definition. The 'weaker' meaning of the term is reserved for a short preliminary period which gets the course underway. The 'stronger' meaning refers to the process of initiating students into independent, self-motivated learning. In the second sense, some see the Intermediate GNVQ as a one-year programme of induction into the Advanced GNVQ.

Ingredients of induction

The lists below identify possible purposes of induction.

Induction to the college or school and its local circumstances

- Introduction to personal tutor. Who does what in the centre – tutor teams.

- Introduction to the range of physical and social facilities at the centre, concentrating on the learning resources (library, workshops, IT-centres, laboratories and so on) and the 'house rules' about their safe use (COSHH, health and safety, fire regulations). Exercises in making use of the full range of these facilities.

- Introduction to the idea of individual action planning. Evaluation of student background, strengths, weaknesses, advice about progression, careers (some understanding of the employment and HE possibilities which are open). National records of achievement.

- Introduction to GNVQ programmes in general.

- Review of the possible combinations of A levels, GCSEs, NVQs and so on which the student could draw on in a complete learning combination.

- Monitoring of students to ensure that they have completed the above elements in the programme.

GNVQ Science induction

A range of activities to:

- introduce action planning, in the first instance in terms of qualifications and experience

- accredit prior achievement

- encourage students to take responsibility for their own work

- encourage students to assess their own performance and progress

- establish group identity given that teamwork should play a large part in GNVQ programmes,

- consolidate basic prior knowledge (for example, from GCSE science)

- outline the GNVQ science specification in a form which does not overwhelm or mystify students – this may have to happen step-by-step.
  - understanding the language of the GNVQ
  - introducing the units, both core skill and mandatory together with some indication of the optional and additional units available (and perhaps how they relate to possible career/HE options)
  - discussing the nature of the knowledge tests and how to prepare for them
- explain the process of assessment, the principle of assembling, keeping, cataloguing and presenting a portfolio of evidence
- outline the grading criteria
- explain other aspects of record keeping for and on the student – including dates and deadlines
- enable students to explore a range of learning styles and reflect on the development of personal learning skills
- introduce students to a range of individual and group 'active-learning' approaches (including structured discussion, reflective/active reading and listening, presenting material to an audience, visits and surveys, role-plays and simulations, use of audio and video recordings, problem-solving, report writing and so on).

Induction activities can include 'ice-breakers', short assignments, and exercises where IT, maths and communication skills are clearly integrated with basic science learning. Introducing the range of activities they may encounter at this stage should stand students in good stead for more elaborate exercises which they will encounter later. As many as possible of these activities should build towards the attainment of one or more mandatory units.

The 'raw' GNVQ specification is not 'student-friendly'. One approach is to give the students the whole specification at the start. Another is to let them build up the specification like a jig-saw (in a logbook); each assignment bringing with it a cover sheet with the related elements and performance criteria.

Many centres like to prepare a brief, introductory leaflet spelling out key features of the GNVQ. You will find an outline of such a leaflet in chapter 2.

During induction students learn about the assessment procedures; they begin to take responsibility for accumulating their evidence portfolios; they start to develop an appropriate range of study skills; and they become generally familiar with GNVQ 'philosophy'.

Diagnosis

'Look out for opportunities to accredit prior learning of core skills.'

For some centres the induction period is an important opportunity to help students make sure that they are on the right style of programme at the right level. This means that the first few weeks must allow opportunities for diagnosis and self-assessment. Hence the need for a 'starter programme' which is worthwhile but does not handicap students who transfer from one course to another at the end. Diagnostic activities can also help to assess the competence of students in core skills.

Team building

Equally important are exercises in team and group formation, examining the most effective combinations of personalities and skills in the formation of a good team. Exercises in team building which help students to evaluate their strengths and weaknesses as team members are a valuable part of induction.

Four models

Nuffield Science in Practice working groups spent several meetings planning induction programmes in the summer of 1993. They came up with several models which many found helpful as starting points when planning their own programmes of work.

MODEL A

'We soon saw the value of induction when a student joined the course late. She missed most of our induction programme and found the first few assignments much more of a struggle than the other students.'

This model is based on the work of the course team at a Surrey sixth form college. The course team started by writing a students' guide to the qualification. This helped to clarify their thinking and to allay their fears. They strongly recommend anyone coming new to GNVQ Science to start in this way – perhaps by modifying the course guide in chapter 2.

The team designed an induction assignment for their Intermediate group to last for about four to five weeks, after a week-or-so's general introduction to college and course. They identified a number of features which they wanted to incorporate into their induction activities. These were that students should have opportunities to:

■ work individually and in groups

■ accumulate evidence and meet the idea of a portfolio

■ carry out research in libraries and data bases

■ carry out record keeping

■ carry out planning and self-assessment thus introducing some of the grading themes

■ review and assess their abilities in core skills

■ go on a visit to give a vocational slant and promote group cohesion

■ make a presentation to the rest of the group.

The team decided to take a central GNVQ theme, 'making things', and set up a series of linked exercises round the topic of Biotechnology, chosen deliberately to avoid any knowledge implications in the mandatory units. This means that students transferring from another course, or joining late, do not lose anything while those taking part definitely gain a great deal in terms of vocational and core skill development.

The course team devised a 'task assessment map' to explain to students the structure of each task, the evidence requirements and the links with the GNVQ specification.

Several good ice-breakers and learning development activities might be integrated into the scheme. These include:

■ getting students to do a safety audit of two labs, one in need of improvement, the other not

■ getting students to work out the principles of safety for themselves by discussing through brainstorming what they would need to do to make a laboratory safe and ensure safe working practice

■ telling students they are laboratory designers with nominal budgets, how would they fit out a safe laboratory?

■ extending the yoghurt practical work to consider colouring agents, preservatives, flavours and so on, from a chemical point of view.

Here is an outline of the assignment which has five main components.

1 Design a biotechnology poster

A task sheet tells students what to do. An assessment map shows how the tasks help students to meet GNVQ Science and core-skill performance criteria (see figure 5.1).

Figure 5.1

TASK ASSESSMENT MAP	V2

By completing the various **Tasks** <u>successfully</u> you will have compiled evidence of achievement in both **Core** and **Science Units**.
The table below shows you which activities in the **Task** cover the various **Performance Criteria** which you need to show you can do for any single **Element**.

It is your responsibility to fill in the page number columns so that evidence of achievement of the individual Performance Criteria can be found easily in your Portfolio of Work.

BIOTECHNOLOGY TASK 2:	Tissue Culture

DEADLINE:	

Science Elems	Perf. Criteria	Activity (opportunities to achieve performance criteria)	Result	Page Nos
1.1		<u>Plan and carry out tasks using standard procedures</u>		
	1-2	A2.2		
	3	A2.2 - Tissue Culture Instruction Sheet (point 5)		
	4	A2.2		
	5	A2.2 (g)		
		<u>Modify standard procedure</u>		
1.2	1	A2.3 (a-f)		
	2	A2.3 plan point (i)		
	3	A2.3 plan points (i-iv)		
	4	A2.3 plan point (iii)		
	5	A2.3 section 5 of report		
	6	A2.3 plan point (iii)		
		<u>Report on a task</u>		
1.3	1-4	A2.3 Practical Report to stated specifications		

Core Elems	Perf. Criteria	Activity (opportunities to achieve performance criteria)	Result	Page Nos
IT 2.1		<u>Set up storage systems and input information</u>		
	1-5	A2.3 Word-processing the report on a floppy disk		
C 2.1		<u>Take part in discussions with a range of people on routine matters</u>		
	1-4	A2.4		
2.2		<u>Prepare written material on routine matters</u>		
	1-4	A2.3		
2.3		<u>Use images to illustrate points</u>		
	1-3	A2.4		
N 2.1		<u>Gather and process data</u>		
	1-6	A2.2 (weighing procedure a-e)		
2.2		<u>Represent and tackle problems</u>		
	1-3	A2.2 (weighing procedure a-e)		
	4	A2.2 (c)		
	5	A2.2 (c-e)		
	6	A2.2 (use of calculator - tutor assessed)		
	7-8	A2.2 (h)		
2.3		<u>Interpret and present data</u>		
	1	A2.2 (h)		
	2	(h - tutor assessed)		
	3	(b-h)		
	4	(h)		
	5-6	(d-h)		

2 Tissue culture

Activity 2.1 What is tissue culture?
Library research based on *Biotechnology* by J. Teasdale.

Activity 2.2 Making a cauliflower tissue culture
A practical activity with full instructions for cloning cauliflower. See *Practical Microbiology and Biotechnology for Schools* by Paul Wymer. Instructions for this activity also appear in *Practical biotechnology* from the National Centre for Biotechnology Education.

▼
▼

Activity 2.3 Investigating the effect of a change on a tissue culture
An investigation planned by students to see how variables influence the growth of cultured cauliflower tissue. Students produce a word-processed report of the activity.

Activity 2.4 Preparing and presenting a short talk
A report on activity 2.3, presented as a short talk.

3 Making yoghurt

Activity 3.1 Making yoghurt and testing for bacteria
Yoghurt making based on the instructions in *Practical Microbiology and Biotechnology for Schools*. (See also *Biotech* from the SSCR Sheffield Biotechnology Group and the SATIS 16–19 unit 34 'Making Yogurt'.) Students record readings in a table on a word-processor.

Activity 3.2 Investigating changes in pH when making yoghurt
This activity uses a pH probe with a data-logger linked to a computer.

4 Making alcohol

Activity 4.1 Making alcohol using free yeast
This provides opportunities to monitor fermentation with an oxygen sensor and pH probe and make density measurements with a hydrometer.

Activity 4.2 Making alcohol using immobilized yeast
Again students monitor the process and determine the yield of alcohol using sensors and a hydrometer.

5 Industrial visit

See chapter 3 in this guide for a section about industry links and the benefits of visits. We will include further guidance to help students benefit from visits in our file of Intermediate assignments.

Our experience of induction helped us to see that we would have to make future assignments much more open-ended to give our students a chance to meet the grading criteria.

This model was developed by our south east regional group with Intermediate GNVQ in mind. The table gives an outline of a programme to last four to five weeks at about 15 hours per week.

Figure 5.2

Week 1	College specific induction Initial action planning (see 'Next five minutes' on page 60) Issue and explain GNVQ Science booklet – later set a quiz on the booklet Explain strategy for keeping a 'logbook' Ice-breaking activity Team building activity (e.g. desert survival, egg races – and others) A social event for staff and students (if appropriate in the centre context) Issue a 'map' of weeks 2–5 and explain how students are expected to build up a portfolio to show the outcomes of this opening unit of work. 'Definitions of science' activity leading to interviews with other students, younger pupils or adults outside the centre. Followed up by 1–2 minute 'quicky' presentations. Self/group-assessment of the 'quicky' presentations (see below under self-assessment)			
Week 2 Week 3 Week 4	**'Tomorrow's World'** (4 hours per week) Students work in groups – they prepare a practical demonstration which they rehearse and later video as a contribution to a topical science TV programme OR They choose an issue to explore and prepare an audio programme on tape about the issue including interviews.	**Science in practice** (5 hours per week) Students find out about local examples of science-based employment: •3 hours (per visit) preparation for one or two half-day visits (hospital, industry, analytical lab, nature reserve and so on). •local and college library and careers room to map out local science based employment.	**Another major activity** (4 hours per week) Possibilities: • 'design-and-make' (could be a measuring instrument or an electronic device), •a local field study, •investigating health and fitness – the start of a year-long program of monitoring building up a data file, •a stimulated public inquiry – linked to a local topical issue.	**Mini-tasks** (2 hours per week) A selection of short review and diagnostic tasks linked to core skills and basic science knowledge (see page 60 for ideas.) Use this to complement the main assignments and to explore the knowledge and skills which students need before embarking on the mandatory units. Include opportunities for paired and group assessment.
Week 5	Evaluation of the video.	Reporting back and evaluation.	Feedback and evaluation.	

You will find that suitable examples of the various activities in the table are listed on page 60 in the classified list of induction components.

These are some other ideas (large and small) which are possible alternatives to activities in figure 5.2.

■ Ask students to devise a science trail around the college or school grounds. Mark out the trail. Prepare a leaflet with commentary and illustrations. Try out the trail with children, students or adults as appropriate.

■ Investigate a science career-line. This could be linked to visits and an exploration of local science-based employment. It could also be part of career action planning.

■ Use 'the nature of science' as a topic – this might include: a case-study from the history of science, the repeat and discussion of a well-known GCSE experiment (What do you see? What generalizations and explanatory theories can help to interpret what you see?), reading two or three topical articles about a current science issue and so on.

■ Investigate the energy loss from a room or laboratory in the centre. Estimate the scale of the loss and its cost. Devise a plan for cutting down energy losses.

■ Introduce activities related to health and safety:
  – 'spot the hazard' – students in a laboratory set up with a range of hazards – students look for them and mark them on a plan of the lab
  – a video of students doing various practical tasks followed by discussion of the health and safety aspects
  – a session with a technician to discuss the ordering, storing and handling materials, equipment and chemicals
  – a case-study of a serious accident (e.g. SATIS 14–16 unit 1003 'A Big Bang' or SATIS 16–19 unit 79 'After Chernobyl').

■ Organize a 'treasure-hunt' in the library or resources centre. Challenge students to find information for a purpose as a way of finding out about the sources of information available to them.

The course team at a school in the West Midlands developed this model as a prelude to an integrated treatment of GNVQ Science.

This is a common induction module for Intermediate and Advanced level. The aims are to:

- introduce and begin to explore the idea of 'what scientists do'
- introduce the GNVQ framework and methods of assessment
- establish group identity
- introduce the styles of working required by GNVQ Science
- introduce the concept of core skills and accredit prior achievement
- emphasize the vocational nature of the course
- begin the process of encouraging students to take responsibility for their own work.

The GNVQ group is timetabled for 4 × 70 minutes sessions per week. In addition the GNVQ group spends about 20 minutes with their tutor on three days of the week. From the start, the students are encouraged to plan their own activities and develop approaches to assignments which match the GNVQ criteria. Students are given increasing responsibility for running the course.

The induction module lasts for three to four weeks and is based on the dairy industry. Figure 5.3 is a chart outlining the main activities.

Figure 5.3

INDUCTION MODULE: THE DAIRY INDUSTRY

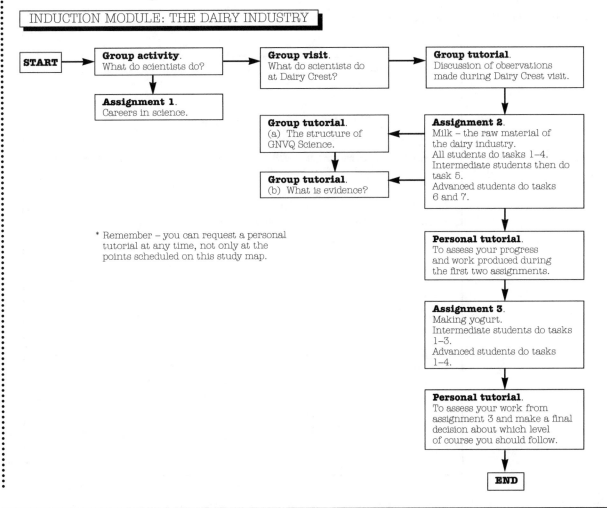

What do scientists do?

Students brainstorm answers to the question 'What do scientists do?' and classify their ideas under the broad headings of 'characterize', 'obtain' and 'control' (see figure 5.4).

Careers in science

Students use the careers library and other sources to research the careers in science open to people with different levels of qualification.

Work-shadowing

Sometime during the first two weeks of the course, pairs of students spend a day work-shadowing a 'scientist' in order to see if the ideas expressed in session 1 about what scientists do agree with what happens in practice. On completion of the work-shadowing students meet as a group to discuss their experiences and review their ideas about what scientists do.

A practical assignment

The practical assignment includes a series of tasks involving 'characterizing', 'obtaining' and 'controlling'.

**Figure 5.4
What do scientists do?
A photocopiable version of
this activity will be included
in the Intermediate
Assignment file**

WHAT DO SCIENTISTS DO?

You have been doing science at school for a number of years so, of course, you know all about what it is that scientists do – but do we all have the same ideas?

1. On the slips of paper provided write down the things that you think scientists do. Use a separate slip of paper for each idea. Concentrate on the general tasks and skills rather than on specific jobs/careers.
   Work by yourself at this stage so that the ideas generated are your own.

2. Get together with 2 or 3 other students and discuss the ideas written on the slips of paper. Do you all agree or are there a wide variety of ideas?
   Get a large sheet of paper and write these three headings across the top:

   Agree   Disagree   Can't decide

   Now use blu-tac to stick the slips under the appropriate heading according to what the group as a whole think about each idea.
   When you have finished display your sheet for other groups to look at. You should take a look at what they have produced. Be prepared to justify your group's decisions to other students.

3. (a) In the light of discussions you may want to change your judgements about some of the ideas on your poster. Do this now.

   (b) Take the list of ideas that you have in the 'agree' column. Can you group any of the ideas together because they are similar in some way? Try to classify your ideas and come up with general titles/headings for each group. Display your classification on the other side of your large sheet of paper and share your ideas with the other groups.

   (c) The team who developed GNVQ Science came up with three broad headings for the things scientists do:

   Characterize

   Obtain

   Control

   Discuss in your group what these words mean. You may wish to check your interpretation using a dictionary or by discussing it with your tutor.

   How do the headings in your classification compare with these?

   Could you place your ideas under these headings?

4. Make a note of your final ideas about what scientists do. During the next week or so you will get the opportunity to observe some scientists at work. It will be interesting to see if you can observe any of your ideas being done in practice.

MODEL C

▼ *continued from page 56*

Core skills

Students begin by analysing their individual strengths and weaknesses and then see how these fit into the core skills framework. They consider what counts as evidence to satisfy the performance criteria and then collect evidence of prior achievement to make a claim for certain core skill elements. At a school they can do this by consulting with their former maths and English teachers and by gathering evidence from their GCSE coursework folders. In this way, students begin to understand what counts as evidence and appreciate what is involved in assembling a portfolio.

MODEL D

This model was developed at a meeting of the North West regional group with both Advanced and Intermediate students in mind. The full programme takes about four weeks. The approach is built around an unofficial unit 0 designed to help students to understand the nature and purpose of the GNVQ specification (see figure 5.5). Even the team who devised this approach were surprised to find how well it worked, particularly with Advanced students. In the light of experience the group would now hold back the introduction of unit 0 until a little later in the induction period.

Support materials

'Introduction to GNVQ' – unit 0 (see figure 5.5)
Ice-breaker activity
Research activity
Laboratory investigation activity
Action plan proforma
Student booklet on action planning, evaluation, record keeping and keeping a logbook.

Outline programme

Activity 1 Ice-breaker
A small-group competition or a role-play (see page 60).

Activity 2 Talk about GNVQ Science
This is based on the 'Introduction to GNVQ Science' outline (see chapter 2). The idea is to get across the language of GNVQ.

Activity 3 A group survey of resources
Students survey the resources available to them to fulfil element 1 of unit 0. This activity can run in parallel with activity 4. Students can use IT to store and present their findings – especially if an introduction to IT features in this phase.

Activity 4 A study-skill task
This can introduce: action planning, keeping a log book, producing a written report in science, monitoring progress, revising for tests and making notes.

▼
▼

Figure 5.5

UNIT 0: INTRODUCTION TO GNVQ SCIENCE

Element 0.1 Determine the resources available to complete a GNVQ assignment successfully

Performance criteria

0.1.1   Human resources available are identified
0.1.2   Physical resources available are identified
0.1.3   Economic and safety constraints are appreciated

Range

Human resources: centre co-ordinator, subject specialists, core-skill consultants, technicians, administrators, librarians, IT co-ordinator, people in a range of local science-based occupations

Physical resources: subject rooms, laboratories, project rooms, IT facilities, libraries, local industry and other places where people use science in their work

Evidence indicators

A report on the resources appropriate to GNVQ students. This may be written but could involve other media

Element 0.2 Demonstrate the characteristics of GNVQ science in the context of a scientific investigation

Performance criteria

0.2.1   An investigation is planned using appropriate resources and facilities
0.2.2   Hazards are identified and a risk assessment completed
0.2.3   Plans are modified in the light of consultation with subject specialists and others
0.2.4   The investigation is carried out, observations and measurements are made
0.2.5   A written report is produced

Range

Standard laboratory apparatus

Evidence indicators

A written report on a short practical investigation

Element 0.3 Establish the characteristics of GNVQ Science

Performance criteria

0.3.1   The structure of the GNVQ specification is understood
0.3.2   The procedures for assessment are understood
0.3.3   Techniques for monitoring progress are identified
0.3.4   The roles of key people involved are defined

Range

Structure	unit (mandatory, core skill, optional and additional), element, performance criteria, range, evidence indicators
Assessment	assignments, evidence indicators, portfolio, test specification, unit tests, merit and distinction grading
Monitoring	action planning, evaluation, techniques of self and group assessment, record keeping
People	Centre co-ordinator, programme co-ordinator, assessor, internal verifier, external verifier

Evidence indicators

'What is GNVQ Science' presented as a poster, talk or audio tape

MODEL D

▼ *continued from page 57*

Activity 5 Working in science
This covers safety rules, risk assessments, common techniques in science and making accurate measurements.

Activity 6 An introductory investigation
This gives experience of: action planning, risk assessment, carrying out an investigation, producing a written report, evaluating an investigation and follow up activities (making notes and answering questions).

Possible investigations:

- investigating suitable materials for a lab coat (Advanced)
- purifying rock salt (Intermediate)
- density variations of salt solutions (Advanced)
- blood transfusion (Advanced).

Activity 7 A study of science at work
There are various possibilites. One approach is for students to make contact with local employers and arrange to interview people who use science in their work. Alternatively students make a study of the employment opportunities for people with science qualifications with the help of the careers service. A third possibility is to invite visiting speakers perhaps with the help of Neighbourhood Engineers or 'Speak Out and Listen'. (See the case studies about working with industry in chapter 4.)

A classified list of induction components

You will find details of the sources on pages 108, 109, 111 and 113 of chapter 10 which ends with an address list.

Action planning

The next five minutes (Gibbs)

Communication skills

A complex problem for copper (Habeshaw and Steeds)
Improve this table (Habeshaw and Steeds)
What's the difference between ...? (Habeshaw and Steeds)
What happened to the gelatin plugs? (Habeshaw and Steeds)
Using the Overhead Projector (Habeshaw and Steeds)
Definitions of science (Habeshaw and Steeds)
Discussion techniques (Centre for Science Education)
Presentation checklist (Centre for Science Education)
Passing on facts (Durham University Business School – *Enterprise in vocational education and training skills development*)
Biotech (SSCR Biotechnology Group)

Ice-breakers

Emptying the bucket (SATIS 16–19 unit 2)
What if...? (SATIS 16–19 unit 27)
Your stars – revelation or reassurance? (SATIS 14–16 unit 907)
Can it be done? Should it be done? (SATIS 14–16 unit 1010)

IT activities

Body data file (Centre for Science Education)

Laboratory activities

Practical Microbiology and Biotechnology for Schools (Wymer)
Biotech (SSCR Biotechnology Group)

Review and diagnosis

Fossil evidence (Centre for Science Education)
States of matter (Centre for Science Education)
Make a SATIS game or puzzle book (SATIS 16–19 unit 53)

Self-assessment

Proformas for self-assessment – chapter 14 in *Active Teaching and Learning Approaches in Science* (Centre for Science Education)
Assessment models (Durham University Business School – *Enterprise in vocational education and training skills development*)
Biotech (SSCR Biotechnology Group)

Speakers

A visiting speaker perhaps from the 'Speak Out and Listen' service supported by the Chemical Industries Association and Understanding British Industry.

Team building exercises

How would you survive? (SATIS unit 404)
Who is everybody? (Durham University Business School – *Enterprise in vocational education and training skills development*)
Biotech (SSCR Biotechnology Group)
Group development section of Asking questions (Durham University Business School – *Enterprise. An educational resource for 14–19 year olds*)
Chemical egg races (Royal Society of Chemistry)

Induction in action

Some centres observe that their students changed dramatically as a result of induction and in the first weeks after it finished. Half way through the autumn term, many students – particularly Advanced students – have a growing sense of personal responsibility and a clear sense of purpose. It is a good sign when, by this stage, students are well enough organized to order their practical materials from the technicians. Much can depend of the 'chemistry' of the group.

Some centres which ran successful induction programmes feel that their students appreciated the chance to get into the swing of GNVQ by doing some work which did not 'count'.

'Looking back I think we gave the students too much information about units, elements, and so on in the first week – they didn't know us well enough to tell us it was going over their heads.'

In the first year of GNVQ Science it was quite common to combine the induction of Intermediate and Advanced groups. This helped colleges to decide on the appropriate level for new students.

An interesting feature of this next case study is a residential field trip which not only provided first-hand experience of 'doing science' but also helped to create 'team spirit'. This technology college has already been running a BTEC National Diploma course and has well established links with industry.

PLANNING INDUCTION AT A COLLEGE IN THE BIRMINGHAM AREA

In the summer term with the new academic year looming a major objective was to devise a suitable induction course. This would provide an introduction to the college, to each other and to teaching and learning approaches to be encountered.

We already had well established procedures for introducing students to the physical and social facilities of the college, based on a previous experience with BTEC National Diploma. We restricted information about the course to a single A4 sheet and we kept GNVQ jargon to an absolute minimum. We adopted as a theme 'the Environment' as the basis of assignments to introduce students to the major types of teaching and learning activity associated with the course. From the start we introduced real, rather than contrived, investigative work with an integrated scientific approach and particularly with a field course component. Fieldwork provided considerable opportunity for teamwork and social bonding.

We chose the Environment as a theme because it dealt with topical and contentious issues familiar to most students and introduced man as a major factor influencing the biotic and abiotic environment. This also served as an introduction to unit 7: Managing living systems.

We decided that we wanted our induction programme to include:

- individual and group work
- practical exercises covering a range of techniques
- practical report writing
- data handling and problem solving exercises
- individual and team presentations in seminars.

It was essential that students should not regard this as some kind of 'bolt on' or ask 'When is the course proper going to begin?', but as a valid introduction to the course. The bonus was that the programme also allowed students to get some science-specific and core-skills performance criteria 'under their belts' at a very early stage, though this was never an integral objective. The field course material was subsequently supplemented with theoretical assignments and more traditional learning methods to complete the 'study of an ecosystem'.

Later, students were introduced to assessment procedures in tutorials based on documentation now accessible to them on their user directories on the computer. We delayed this introduction until the end of the first half term when students had found their feet and were confident that they had successfully negotiated the transition from pre- to post-16 education.

▼ *continued from page 62*

An outline of the environment study

Part 1: Environmental issues
Time allocation: 50 hours.

We built this study round four topics drawing on various published sources including Salters Advanced Chemistry and the Science in the Environment project from the University of York Science Education Group.

Table 5.1
CORE SKILLS

	Core skill		
	Communication	**Application of number**	**IT**
Assignment 1.1: The ozone layer	+	−	−
Assignment 1.2: The greenhouse effect	+	−	−
Assignment 1.3: Acid rain	+	+	+
Assignment 1.4: Motor vehicle emissions	+	+	−

Part 2: Marine ecology at St David's, Pembrokeshire
Time allocation: 30 hours

This comprised two assignments: 2.1 The ecology of rocky shores and 2.2 The ecology of sand dunes.

We chose sites to provide a variety of activities.

■ An introduction to sampling techniques.

■ Different methods for the recording of ecological data.

■ Species identification and production of keys.

■ Monitoring the affects of freshwater on the distribution of marine organisms.

■ Measurement of chloride ions, by titration, from rockpools at intervals above low water or as affected by river water.

■ Assessment of the affect of external influences on an ecosystem. In this instance a sewage works provided an opportunity to introduce aseptic techniques and 'identification' of coliforms using standard microbiological techniques alongside appropriate data.

Assessment and record keeping

A claiming culture

A key feature of any GNVQ is the need for students to take responsibility for negotiating and participating in each stage of a planning-learning-assessment-review cycle.

'Make a priority of getting your assessment and recording system organized.'

As the staff at one college put it, the aim is to build up a 'claiming culture' which puts the onus on students to demonstrate that they have met the performance criteria. Students have to compile and index a portfolio of evidence which maps their work onto the performance criteria and range.

Figure 6.1

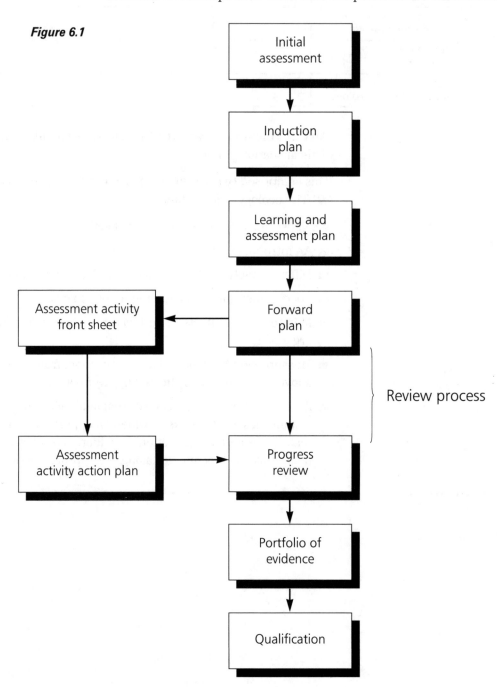

There is, however, no escape from the need for teachers or tutors to spend time with individual students to assess performance and to check coverage of the elements. Some centres choose to allocate a small group of students to each member of the course team. The staff member then ensures that documentation is being properly filled in. Another approach is to timetable tutorial time for this purpose with one member of staff taking on the full responsibility for the whole class. In the early stages this can be very time consuming. Pilot centres report that a tutorial allocation of two hours per week can be inadequate even with a group of only a dozen students.

Accreditation of prior learning (APL)

One or two colleges have an APL verifier in the science school and see opportunities for giving credit for achievement in:

- tasks completed at work outside the college

- other vocational courses

- GCSE coursework.

Right from the start of the course many centres try to put the onus on students to take evidence of achievement to a tutor for logging.

Building portfolios

Most students carry a working file in which they keep notes, guidance and ongoing records. From time to time they transfer completed work to their portfolios. Only the students' own work goes into the portfolio and only that part of their work which contributes directly to the evidence that they have met the performance criteria and covered the range.

Students have the responsibility for indexing and cross-referencing their portfolios so that assessors and verifiers can check the coverage of performance criteria and range dimensions. The growing portfolio must be free-standing and self-explanatory.

Students have to learn how to build up a portfolio and here we include the advice which one college gives to its Intermediate students. The college works within the BTEC framework for assessment.

Figure 6.2

BUILDING YOUR PORTFOLI

To achieve success in GNVQ Intermediate level you need to build up a portfolio of evidence to show that you have achieved the performance criteria.

You have to show us your ability to work in a scientific manner in a range of situations across all areas of science. This is far more demanding than a GCSE course because so much more is left to you to organize and plan in terms of the day-to-day completion of your assignments.

When you achieve all the performance criteria of the four mandatory units plus at least two additional units you will have accumulated all the evidence necessary for the award of a GNVQ, so long as you have reached level 2 in the core skill units.

Of course you have to pass a test in each mandatory unit, but this does not affect your overall grade.

Whether you are awarded a pass, merit, or distinction, is determined by the quality of work in your portfolio alone.

What type of evidence will my portfolio contain?

Your portfolio will contain your highest achievements in the various elements.

The evidence may consist of some of the following:

- industry/market surveys
- plans for organizing investigations or events
- project work, case studies, assignments, projects, reports
- diagrams, graphs, photographs
- role-play activities
- computer based outputs
- letters of validation (to state you have certain competencies)
- accounts of routine activities in the lab or workplace
- models, drawings, and so on
- certificates or prizes from other sources.

The portfolio must be organized and cross-referenced so that your tutors and any external assessor can see exactly where to find the evidence that you have met all the performance criteria for every element of each unit.

How do I make sure my portfolio is properly organized?

Your tutor will give you guidance on this at regular review meetings. In addition various sheets are issued with assignments and at reviews to help organize your work.

These sheets are:

An activity action plan – to help you plan for an activity. Your tutor can help you fill it out. You should have one for each major activity.

An activity information sheet – which shows the units, elements and performance criteria you can achieve in an assignment, and tells you how to do it. You must attach one of these sheets to each piece of assignment work in your portfolio.

Activity information feedback – completed by your tutors before they hand work back to you. Tutors 'sign off' the performance criteria you have met successfully and give you help with any that have not been met. You must attach one to each assignment in your portfolio.

Progress review form – used by you and your tutor during counselling sessions. It monitors your overall progress. It is used as an index for a subsection of the portfolio.

Forward plan – completed as a result of a progress review. This helps you to plan activities for the next phase of the learning programme.

Unit tracking record – this goes at the front of your portfolio and acts as an overall index so that the external verifier can quickly locate the evidence you have to meet any particular performance criteria.

Guide to performance – this records occasions where your performance has been at merit or distinction level. By the end of your course it will be complete and will be used to determine your overall grade.

At the front of your portfolio you should also include:

Current assessment record – which records your achievements at entry to the course.

Induction plan – which identifies activities right at the start of the course, and confirms what mandatory, optional, and additional units you are taking.

Learning and assessment plan – which helps you identify current activities, and plan future progress.

Who is responsible for keeping my portfolio in order?

You are! But if you are not sure what to do at any stage just ask your personal tutor during one of your review meetings.

Storing portfolios

Science departments generally provide a central base where students can store their portfolio of evidence. This may be a filing cabinet in a staff room, laboratory or tutor base. One or two colleges have set aside a room for the purpose with shelves and box files. Some centres aim to prevent plagiarism by keeping portfolios under lock-and-key and restricting access to periods when there are staff present.

Other centres regard student responsibility for looking after portfolios as an essential part of GNVQ and simply retain a photocopy of the tracking documentation as a safeguard in case a portfolio, or part of it, goes missing.

All agree that students have the responsibility for building up the evidence. One or two larger colleges have appointed part-time support staff to manage the exercise of collating and recording assessment data with the help of computers.

Tests on the mandatory units

The external tests on the mandatory units are minimum hurdles. Though relatively unimportant compared to the portfolio of evidence, they are mastery tests with a 70 per cent pass mark.

Some GNVQ units do not lend themselves to external testing. In the pilot year this meant that there were no tests on unit 1 Intermediate and unit 8 Advanced. All other mandatory units were tested.

Tests last an hour and in that time students enter responses to 30 to 40 objective-test items by filling in a machine-markable form. This makes it possible for the awarding bodies to report the marks within 30 days.

The format agreed for the test specifications divides each unit into a series of focuses. This style was agreed to suit the first five GNVQs. In the pilot year the science working group found the notion of focuses unnecessary and so in the science specifications the focuses correspond to elements.

Grading

Students who show a level of performance above the basic level can gain a merit or distinction award. Students have to pass all the required units before they can be considered for a higher grade. At Intermediate level grading is assessed on the basis of the students' ability at planning, information seeking and information handling. At Advanced level they also have to meet criteria for evaluation.

The mode of assessment and model of progression built into GNVQ Science can be very encouraging to some students. Many staff at pilot centres are confident that they will have the nucleus of an Advanced level group from those who have spent a year on GNVQ Intermediate. There are encouraging examples from colleges running BTEC First and National Diploma programmes to show how students who have performed badly at GCSE can, given time and encouragement, gain confidence and work through successfully to a standard which equips them to move on to employment or higher education.

GNVQ grading is based on the best third of the students' portfolios which means that they can steadily build up their competence at planning, information handling and evaluation during the early part of the programme and not be penalized for taking time to do so.

Assessors and verifiers

Assessors have to learn the art of giving constructive feedback to students as they build their portfolios. From an early stage students have to get a feeling for not only the basic requirements of performance criteria and range but also the expectations of the merit and distinction gradings.

Internal verifiers should have some subject expertise so that they can take a leading role in co-ordinating and managing the assessment team. Pilot centres advise that regular meetings of assessors and the internal verifier help to establish common standards.

TDLB assessor and verifier awards

Acronyms and codes are rampant in the world of vocational qualifications. If you can decode the initials TDLB and distinguish D32 from D35 you are already on the way to mastering the jargon. One benefit of the system of accrediting assessors and verifiers is that in the process teachers and lecturers experience building a portfolio of evidence which helps to make everyone more sympathetic to the pressures on students.

Walsall TVEI have written a helpful booklet describing in some detail the roles and responsibilities of GNVQ assessors (see chapter 10). The awards were first devised for NVQ assessment and the value of the Walsall booklets is that they reinterpret the awards for GNVQ.

The TDLB is the Training and Development Lead Body which is responsible for the standards for training. These are the relevant qualifications for people concerned with GNVQ.

D32   The assessor award – direct observation of student achievement

D33   The assessor award – credit for achievement from activities in which the assessor is not directly involved

D34   The internal verifier award

D35   The external verifier award

D36   Accreditation of prior learning counsellor award

All this seems very formal so here is an account from a lecturer at a college in the east of England, describing what it feels like to go through the process of gaining the qualifications.

THE EXPERIENCE OF GNVQ ASSESSOR AND INTERNAL VERIFIER TRAINING

GNVQ this! GNVQ that! What's it all about, I wondered. I thought I had better investigate further. The first stage was to meet other people involved in the GNVQ scheme. Fortunately, I'd heard about a training session that was being organized by the college, so I promptly signed up.

With trepidation, I attended the one day course. To my surprise I met other people all in the same situation, which was comforting. The light at the end of the tunnel had been switched on. Pity it had only a 40 W light bulb. The course tutor, Sheila, entered the room with a big smile and even bigger stack of folders. (Someone switched the light off!) We were given a folder, which on completion of the course would become a 'portfolio', and a booklet containing units describing D32, D33 and D34.

After the first training session the folder still looked very bare and very empty! However, the light at the end of the tunnel was beginning to glow brighter – 60 W now!

Eager to learn more, I attended several science meetings given by the Royal Society of Arts and Nuffield Science in Practice. I was accumulating plenty of ideas and materials suitable for my portfolio. Gradually, the crystal ball was starting to clear and I was beginning to understand what 'performance criteria' meant together with the rest of the jargon.

My enthusiasm was becoming increasingly obsessive. I would be in the bath at home and EUREKA! I'd thought of another piece of evidence for my portfolio. Students were harangued into giving me examples of their work.

Within a couple of weeks I had enough material clipped into my folder to warrant an 'interim assessment' with my tutor.

The interview went really well. At first, I was apprehensive. Had I accumulated enough material? Was it relevant? Did it fulfil the requirements for D32, D33 and D34? Sheila explained to me that the main aim of the interim assessment was to ensure I was pursuing the correct path and gathering the necessary information. I explained how I had proceeded. It was reassuring to find my ideas correlating with Sheila's expectations. Sheila gave me further excellent advice. In particular I must remember to focus on three vocational students, as per D33. Bearing this in mind the light at the end of the tunnel was decidedly brighter.

Back at home I curled up in my favourite armchair with a cup of decaffeinated, sugar-free coffee and a pack of chocolate biscuits (well one deserves a break from the diet occasionally) and sketched out three student assessment plans.

At college I raided my students' work and fashioned it into my plans. This included project work, experimental write-ups, assignments and work experience reports. Terrific! D33 almost complete. The work for D32 needed a small amount of evidence on top of that.

I began to collect material for D34, including student grade-sheets, minutes of team meetings, course guidelines and so on. At this point, I took a step back to review my progress. I could not believe how much I'd achieved. Putting all the evidence into the portfolio made me realize just how much effort goes into running the course. It had taken me three weeks from having an empty portfolio to seeing it in all its glory – bulging at the seams. The light at the end of the tunnel was shining brightly now.

The day of the final assessment was upon me. I met Sheila on the steps and she informed me the interview would not be in the usual room, the only room available was the Medical Room. (The light was beginning to flicker. Had I done something wrong – PANIC!). Fortunately, all went well.

Sheila reviewed the evidence I'd collected, asked me questions about it and quizzed me about my understanding of GNVQs.

Then it was over. Successfully completed.

I came out of the tunnel and into the fresh air! That called for a celebration. I dashed to the local cake shop and bought the stickiest doughnut ever made and wolfed it down!

This is the one and only case where I didn't want to leave one crumb of evidence.

How do we keep the whole process manageable?

'Students really don't like all the record keeping – especially early on when they have not got the hang of all the forms. After a while they get into the swing of things but it's not something they enjoy.'

It is all too easy to be swamped by the process of tracking achievement. The whole business can rapidly become a nightmare. Filling in grid sheets of performance can become obsessive and distracting. Finding time to complete logbooks is also an issue.

The awarding bodies publish schemes for tracking and record keeping but some of the suggestions are proving over elaborate. Centres are learning to be highly selective and beginning to customize the paperwork to make it manageable.

Some centres have found it helpful to consult colleagues with experience of running other GNVQs such as Business or Health and social care. During the first round of pilots, some centres were criticized for putting too much emphasis on written reports. There is much to be said for a variety of evidence collected with the help of checklists, oral questioning and observation – or even audio and video tapes.

Some colleges are working towards a common pattern of documentation across all GNVQ programmes. There is a danger that this will become over elaborate and not meet the needs of particular programmes. It is clearly important that the documentation helps the students as much as possible, rather than meeting only the needs of teaching or administrative staff.

The golden rule is to keep the number of different forms to an absolute minimum. Look out for forms which nobody refers to again once they have been filled in – reject them. Finally, do not forget the need for time to complete the lengthy process of internal verification that somehow has to be timetabled into the students' programme.

Getting the paperwork right is one of the key steps to success. Here is an example to show how one college approached the problem.

TAMING THE PAPERWORK AT A COLLEGE IN THE MIDLANDS

Our initial problem with GNVQ records was trying to anticipate what was required. Early attempts to design standard forms soon changed in the light of experience. We will probably have to change them again as data accumulates. It is not possible to do it any other way. Unless you have very specific needs and are clear what they are, it is very easy to include things which are irrelevant and to miss bits that are needed.

From our point of view the standard forms produced by our awarding body seem to be the proverbial committee-generated camel. Forms designed by ourselves to do exactly what we need are much more likely to be used. Others are resisted and resented.

We have now standardized on three main sets of files, one to keep course administration including single copies of all assignments, one to keep records of assessments including grading criteria and one for records of core skills.

We have standard forms for recording performance criteria and range in the form of 'tick' lists – one per student and a master to check which assignments cover which skill. We also have a standard form to record grading criteria and one for each core skill.

Finally, we have several versions of a cover sheet which is attached to the front of assignments on which we record – for the students – the criteria, range, core skills and grading criteria results.

Choosing an awarding body?

As a project we work with all three awarding bodies. Centres linked to the three bodies come to our meetings. All we can do to help here is to point out the main criteria which centres consider when making their choice. These are:

■ established links, if any, with an awarding body

■ the advantage of having all GNVQs with the same body

■ the quality of service

■ cost and

■ the nature of the optional and additional units.

The next case study, from a sixth form college in Surrey, discusses the advantages and disadvantages of devising a logbook to help students track and record their achievements.

GNVQ SCIENCE – ASSESSING AND RECORDING COMPETENCE

At the first meeting of our GNVQ team we become aware that assessment and record keeping would be a demanding task. The key sentence that comes at the bottom of every element is: 'Evidence will also show that the candidate understands the performance criteria in respect to all the items in the range'. The consequence of this demand is that a student's portfolio must contain all this evidence in addition to the specific evidence indicators of each element. We decided that it would be an enormous task to record and retain all the students' work in a way that would be accessible to our internal or external verifier.

The way forward seemed to be to place the emphasis of recording on the students. However, they would need clear guidance on what to record and retain in their portfolio. We chose to produce a student logbook.

Figure 6.3 A sample page from the logbook

Initial Assessment

> **Career Goal**
>
>
>
> **Qualification details** – subjects and date
>
>
>
>
>
> **Work experience**
>
>
>
> **Other achievements**
>
>

Core skills assessment

Communication	Improving own learning and performance
Application of number	Working with others
Information Technology	Problem solving

Need of specialist help

Student signature:	Tutor signature:
	Date:

The logbook was produced in a series of sections which gave the student all the information they could need about the GNVQ scheme. The first few pages gave a broad introduction to the course and laid out how we expected them to use the logbook. They were also given the criteria for grading. There then followed a page for their initial assessment.

We recruited thirteen students on to our Intermediate GNVQ and three staff were involved in the teaching. We therefore decided that each member of staff would take special responsibility for the initial assessment of four or five students and follow through the monitoring of their progress. The initial assessment provided a useful opportunity for staff and students to meet and discuss the students' hopes and aspirations. The log also contains pages for progress reviews at halfway through and the end of each term.

The main part of the logbook consists of the detailed requirements of each unit. One page is given over to each element and on a facing page is a blank table for students to fill in as they complete assignments. The table provides space for them to list both the range they have covered and the performance criteria. Initially we had planned to record only the main evidence indicators, but as the implications of 'all the items in the range' became apparent we decided all assignments should be logged and all that were of acceptable standard should be retained in the portfolio. At first students found it difficult to take responsibility for recording and needed considerable guidance through the first few weeks of the course.

One advantage of this system is that all work can be cross-referenced and some items of range can be covered once but recorded against more than one element, and we anticipate students being able to do this retrospectively. We have chosen to leave the optional units until the end of the course, and at first we only issued students with a log for the mandatory units and the core skills.

When we issue a log for the optional units it will be possible for students to claim they have covered some items of the range in earlier units. For example, flame tests for sodium potassium, calcium and copper appear in RSA's pilot optional unit 8 'Earth science' and may be covered in unit 2 'Explore materials'. The performance criteria are sufficiently close to allow considerable overlap.

There are many other opportunities for this form of cross-referencing and we have decided to cover the whole of Intermediate unit 1 'Work on scientific tasks' in this integrated way. The possibilities for integration of units have become more apparent as we have become more familiar with the course specifications.

The student log also contains the core-skill specifications. We decided to give our students the performance criteria for both Intermediate and Advanced in the hope that some would work towards the higher level, or at least have some credit to carry on to an Advanced level course next year. They have been given the responsibility for claiming credit in core skill units. Once again they have found this difficult as it means constantly referring to this part of the log. At our review times this has been a major task. However, many are now, after about a term, rising to the task and presenting work and claiming credit.

▼ *continued from page 74*

Internally we will accept a tutor-cert~
for accreditation of prior learning a~
for this purpose irrespective of w~
science or changes to another G~
Intermediate non-mandatory ~
able to claim credit in these ~

When students are given ~
sheet and an assessment shee~
partially completed by the tutor in~
criteria that should be covered. When s~
responsibility to fill in the assessment sheet ~
tutor's expected outcomes and any additional area~
covered. If the tutor agrees the items are entered in the ~
the staff. The planning sheet can be used as evidence towar~

Figure 6.4a Sample planning and assessment sheets

Example Assignment Planning Sheet
General National Vocational Qualification
Science Intermediate Level

Activity Action Plan: *Assignment Title*   Student Name:

What do I need to find out?	What do I need to do?	In which order?	By when?	What amendments do I need to make?

Tutor comment

Figure 6.4b

75

Example Assignment Assessment Sheet
General National Vocational Qualification
Science Intermediate Level

Assignment title:
The properties of a material used in construction

Range covered	**Evidence indicators**
Properties: tensile strength, density, elasticity, chemical attack. Uses: construction materials Structure of the chosen material Safety: all care taken and where appropriate COSHH and HASAWA taken into account.	Report on the properties of the material and how this influences its use in construction.

Performance criteria	**Mandatory core**	**Non mandatory core**
2.2.1 Potential hazards of work identified 2.2.2 Properties are determined 2.2.3 Safety procedures are carried out 2.2.4 Use of material matched to property 2.2.5 Property related to structure 1.3.1 Data collected using standard method 1.3.2 Data displayed in required form 1.3.3 Outcome of task compared with information from secondary sources 1.3.4 Valid conclusions are drawn	**Communication:** 2.2.1 All necessary information included is accurate 2.2.2 Documents legible 2.2.3 Grammar and spelling correct 2.2.4 Appropriate format **Number** 2.2 Represent and tackle problems at level 2 **Information Technology** 2.1 Set up storage and input information	**Problem solving** 2.1 Use established procedures to clarify routine plans 2.2 Select standard solutions to routine problems

Student comment	**Tutor's feedback**

Date	**Student signature**	**Tutor signature**

The main disadvantage of the log has been the cost. By giving each student the full structure of the course in a curly plastic binder with a protective plastic cover we have spent just over £3 per student and the optional units will add a further cost. The second problem is that we have virtually no record of achievement if students lose their logs. To reduce the chance of loss the logs are retained in college. However, the log is a profile of student achievement and we must decide whether to allow students to take them home for parental inspection prior to a consultation evening. Logic says we should as it would be pointless for students and tutors to produce another document containing the same information. The main safeguard for the log is that students realize its importance in their development and as evidence for a verifier.

What makes a science qualification vocational?

An awkward word

The word at the heart of NVQ and GNVQ is vocational. But what does it actually mean?

The primary meaning of **vocation** is a divine call to a career or occupation. Such calls are rare in a secular society and the weaker meaning of the word as an employment, trade or profession seems more appropriate. Therefore 'vocational' must be anything to do with such employment and a 'vocational qualification' must be one which prepares aspirants for their chosen employments, trades or professions. What could be more straightforward?

At least two problems immediately arise. First, is there any difference between vocational education and vocational training? Second, what exactly is the employment, trade or profession of science?

Vocational education and training

Most people would probably agree that differences between education and training are largely artificial. Indeed, the dictionary defines education as a subdivision of training in intellectual and moral principles.

Nevertheless, the two words often conjure up very different images. Traditionally, education was a preparation for the professions who think, manage and govern while training was for tradespeople and operatives who made products or provided services under the control of the cadre of professionals.

Such social distinctions are long out-of-date, but the damaging imagery sometimes lingers on. Education still looks down on training. 'Vocational' attaches in many people's minds to 'training', and the phrase 'vocational education' is mentally translated into 'vocational training'. Most teachers and students prefer 'academic' courses, no matter how inappropriate, rather than anything 'vocational', because this conjures up a picture of a training in basic skills with little factual content or intellectual rigour.

Much good work has nevertheless been done in vocational education but there has also been a great deal of under-resourced, low-grade 'training' for dead-end jobs among the under-employed, with the accompanying perception that they are to blame for their own fate. While it is true that too many young people do under-achieve at school and lack essential qualifications and skills, they can see that whatever skills they can realistically hope to acquire, there are no jobs for them to take up.

Some of the negative attitudes unfairly associated with this 'new vocationalism' became attached, with even less justification, to the vocational education programmes run by BTEC, RSA and City and Guilds before they became providers of GNVQs. In science the only viable vocational alternative to A level science for sixth formers has been the BTEC National Diploma. Universities and employers are increasingly aware of the virtues of this qualification but the numbers studying for it remain very small.

Most of those who enrol on full-time BTEC National Diploma courses do so by default. Many cannot get onto the A level programme of their choice and only then discover that they have an alternative. BTEC Diploma students (and to a lesser extent their part-time, day-release colleagues on BTEC National Certificates) generally have to accept the prevalent cultural opinion that vocational courses and vocational students are inferior to their academic counterparts.

Part of the mission of any teacher or lecturer involved with GNVQ is to overcome the connotation of inferiority which is too easily linked with the word 'vocational'. The first step in the process is to recognize that the prejudice exists and to expect, and be ready to counter, cynicism about the quality and value of vocational qualifications which exists in some quarters.

What is the vocation of science?

How do we define the particular vocation 'science'. What is this particular employment, trade or profession and what do scientists actually do?

One answer is that scientists use their intellectual and practical investigative skills to carry out research which increases the depth and scope of the body of proven knowledge about nature. The work is done for the most part in laboratories and libraries and scientists are logical thinkers, skilled observers, and proficient designers and operators of sophisticated instruments and apparatus.

What is the appropriate vocational qualification for this pure research stereotype? It needs to concentrate on acquiring and using intellectual and practical skills and on learning large parts of the existing body of knowledge, while at the same time encouraging reflection and curiosity.

This is exactly the education and training programme which has evolved for pure scientists over the past 150 years. In its modern form, an intensive two-year science and maths A level course is followed by a three year single honours science degree, topped off with a further three years of postgraduate research for a PhD. Science A levels are therefore highly vocational as well as academic qualifications for anyone aspiring to do basic scientific research.

The trouble with this model is that basic research represents only a tiny fraction of the employment opportunities open to scientifically qualified people. Is A level science a suitable starting qualification for the much larger body of students aiming for less rarified and specialized scientific employment?

It is even open to question whether the traditional academic route is still the appropriate preparation for a career in basic research. It is becoming clear that success in research does not simply depend on a combination of keen intellect, technical skill and knowledge of a large amount of fact and theory. Other skills and different sorts of knowledge are needed, which many current A level and science degree programmes do not provide.

To improve student preparation for the vocation of science, two things are necessary: a quantitative assessment of what the employment opportunities in science are and a qualitative picture of what people in scientific posts actually do. When the RSA working committee on Science GNVQ, chaired by Dr Ken Gadd, set out to design the new specifications at the end of 1992 there were no clear answers to either of these questions. Research had started but the results were not available in time to inform the pilot specifications for GNVQ Science.

The research results were published in 1993 as *Mapping the science, technology and mathematics domain*, in the form of a Report from the Science Qualifications Task Force of the Council of Science and Technology Institutes (CSTI). This is an umbrella organization representing the main professional bodies of scientists, including the bodies responsible for guiding the development of GNVQ Science.

The CSTI commissioned this report as part of its effort to be accepted as the effective Lead Body for the setting of occupational standards (and hence NVQ design) for the employment sector of science. The report was partly funded by the Department of Employment in sympathy with this objective. Because a central forum for such standards is missing, an *ad hoc* series of occupational standards and NVQs are emerging in some sectors of science employment, notably technical work in the chemical and pharmaceutical industries.

The CSTI report makes extremely interesting reading. Its conclusions indicate that the current academic pattern of preparation for work in science may be wrong and that the specification of GNVQ Science may not have moved far enough from the old academic model to be an entirely suitable alternative or replacement.

The Report first of all establishes the extent of current scientific employment. It divides science-based employment into three main categories.

- **Main** – defined as those areas where the practice of science, technology and/or mathematics is the main activity of those employed.
- **Critical** – defined as those areas where the main occupational function is not exclusively science, technology and/or mathematics but where the knowledge, understanding or practice of science, technology and/or mathematics is critical to occupational competence.
- **Enhanced** – defined as those where the main occupational function is not science, technology and/or mathematics but where the knowledge, understanding or practice of science, technology and/or mathematics enhances occupational competence.

There is also a fourth category of occupations in which there are some individuals for whom science, technology or mathematics is a **significant** (perhaps somewhere between critical and enhanced) part of their competence. This last category is only needed because the data base used to compile the statistics in the report classifies jobs under only a single heading. Therefore some occupations where many people need scientific competence are classified in a non-scientific group. For example, 106 000 secondary-education teachers appeared in the 'significant' category because the classification 'teacher' includes larger numbers who teach non-scientific subjects.

The overall numbers involved here are large. The **main** occupation category contains about 0.6 million people (such as chemists, laboratory technicians, and medical radiographers), the **critical** category another 1.7 million (including doctors, nurses, dentists and engineers), the **enhanced** group nearly another million (farm managers, hairdressers, food and chemical process workers are featured here) while a final 0.5 million appeared in the group who needed science as a **significant** part of their competence (with the secondary-school teachers mentioned above and members of such professions as technical sales representatives and production managers). The technical difficulties with job classification mean that these figures are only approximate. Nevertheless the total figure of about 3.8 million employees is impressive, even though the estimate is subject to a large margin of error.

Looking at the quantitive data another way, the following table shows the rank order of the main occupational groups featured in the report (excluding IT, mathematics and one or two other categories). Table 7.1 does not appear in the report but was compiled from it.

Table 7.1

Occupational group	Number (thousands)	Category
Nurses and midwives	467	critical
Agriculture/horticulture/forestry/fisheries	329	enhanced/significant
Engineers (of all types)	311	critical
Chem/gas/petroleum process operatives	161	enhanced
Medical doctors and dentists	156	critical
Laboratory science technicians	130	main
Medically related occupations (e.g. radiographers, opticians, physiotherapists, chiropodists, occupational therapists)	128	main/critical
Food processing operatives (drink/food/tobacco)	113	enhanced
Secondary school science teachers	106	significant
Product, works and maintenance managers	86	significant
Marketing sales managers	73	significant
University/HE/FE teaching professionals	64	main
Engineering technicians	60	critical
Biological scientists and biochemists	49	main
Chemists	39	main
Physicists, geologists, meteorologists and other natural scientists	28	main

If these figures had been available to the RSA development group, the pilot GNVQ Science specifications might have turned out rather differently. For instance, the domination of scientific employment by the health care professions might have led to more than half of one Advanced pilot mandatory unit devoted to human biology. More radically, the specification could have focused more clearly on the needs of students who will eventually become nurses, horticulturalists or laboratory technicians rather than continuing to reflect the academic framework of the science disciplines. To be fair, RSA did consider scientific occupational themes as a basis for the mandatory units but decided against it.

However, Professor Dick West, writing in the *Times Educational Supplement* on 24 September 1993 suggested that it would have been sensible to design vocational Science GNVQ round occupational theme-based questions such as, 'How and in what ways is scientific knowledge used and applied in our society and how is it used by different groups?'

Dick West proposed that to analyse these important social, economic and political questions we also need a sound understanding of scientific context. By switching the context away from the science of scientists – a context of little appeal to many students – to that of medicine, engineering, productive industry, care of the environment, nursing, child development and childcare and so on, we could create an approach to advanced level studies that is distinctively novel and essentially useful.

But the huge diversity of occupational contexts for science does make it difficult to find common vocational threads which might inform a single set of GNVQ Science unit specifications. One solution, at least for the 'main' and 'critical' groups in the CSTI categories is to ask the question, 'What do scientists do?' This was the question the RSA working committee eventually used as a basis for designing the GNVQ mandatory specifications.

The RSA working committee's answers to the question were framed largely in instrumental terms. The members of the committee identified three generic themes of scientific action and designed the mandatory units round them. They were:

■ making, building and synthesizing

■ characterizing, analysing and identifying

■ monitoring, controlling, managing and regulating.

The CSTI's answer to the question 'What do scientists do?' was more radical. Their full framework is an elaborate branching map to show the many different ways in which people use science at work. Figure 7.1 shows the overarching categories in the CSTI framework.

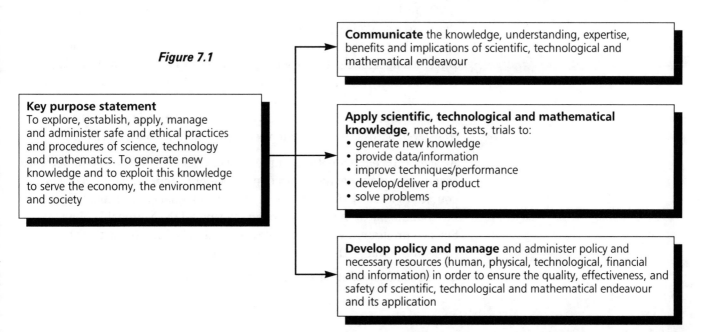

Figure 7.1

Key purpose statement
To explore, establish, apply, manage and administer safe and ethical practices and procedures of science, technology and mathematics. To generate new knowledge and to exploit this knowledge to serve the economy, the environment and society

Communicate the knowledge, understanding, expertise, benefits and implications of scientific, technological and mathematical endeavour

Apply scientific, technological and mathematical knowledge, methods, tests, trials to:
• generate new knowledge
• provide data/information
• improve techniques/performance
• develop/deliver a product
• solve problems

Develop policy and manage and administer policy and necessary resources (human, physical, technological, financial and information) in order to ensure the quality, effectiveness, and safety of scientific, technological and mathematical endeavour and its application

The 'key purpose statement' contains the basic *raison d'etre* of pure scientific research, 'to generate new knowledge', but what is interesting is how much more it contains. Apart from the obvious extensions to applying and exploiting knowledge there are terms such as 'service', 'ethical practice', 'environment and society', aspects of being a scientist which are not addressed by the traditional academic science menu of developing technical expertise and learning an abstract body of knowledge.

To achieve this key purpose, the CSTI framework suggests that individuals working with science need expertise in three areas. Knowledge and skills about doing science is only one of them. Equally important are communication and management skills. Communication and management are not subservient to science knowledge. The important message here is that these skills should be developed more overtly in a wider education and training for young scientists.

Nuffield Science in Practice publications will try to take account of this wider interpretation of 'what scientists do' and the variety of contexts in which scientific knowledge is used. We will draw in examples to illustrate the diverse ways in which scientific knowledge is used an applied in our society.

We have identified several strands which we think should be woven into GNVQ programmes, some of which overlap with the core skills units common to all GNVQs.

We will not deal with these themes in a generalized or theoretical way. This is not appropriate for the students we have in mind. Our approach is to seek out representative case studies. The contexts we use will not only introduce mainstream scientific ideas but also examine the professional role of people who use science in their work. Some of these professional themes are outlined in figure 7.2.

Vocational science programmes in practice

Quite apart from the content and context differences which might distinguish a vocational post-16 science course from an 'academic' one, there are also pedagogic issues. The specification for GNVQ Science follows the patterns established for vocational BTEC First and National Diplomas in Science. The teaching, learning and assessment frameworks of BTEC courses were already very different from those of A level and it is clear that both students and teaching staff saw many positive features in courses based on the vocational BTEC model. Many of these virtues have transfered across from existing vocational programmes into GNVQ.

At one of the early meetings of the Nuffield Science in Practice project, we asked a group of teachers with experience of running vocational science courses to identify the important features of a quality vocational programme. Most of them had been offering BTEC National Diploma Science programmes in their colleges or schools. The following list gives some of the things they particularly valued.

■ The absence of all-or-nothing terminal exams.

Figure 7.2

USING AND APPLYING SCIENCE IN SOCIETY

How, where and why scientists work
- Careers open to people with scientific qualifications.
- The pleasures and rewards of a career in science and technology.
- How and where scientists are employed – their place in hierarchies/management structures.
- The wider context of a scientist's work: social, economic and environmental implications.
- The professional organizations to which scientists belong.
- Professional values and attitudes.

Reading and writing about science and technology
- Ways in which scientific and technical knowledge is published: research papers, abstracts, research reviews, textbooks.
- Routes from the world of science to the wider public via the media.
- Freedom of information. Restrictions on the publication of information. The right of individuals to privacy – including medical and other personal data.

Innovation
- The relationship between research and development.
- Factors which may promote or hinder effective innovation.
- Creativity and teamwork.
- Factors influencing the commercial success of innovations.
- The notion of appropriate technology.
- Patents as a source of information about invention and innovation. Reasons for patenting inventions. Limitations to the patenting system.
- The importance of design.
- The contrast between a 'scientific/mathematical' approach to tackling problems and an engineering approach.

Industrial production and its regulation
- The scale and diversity of science-based industry in the UK.
- Economic, social and environmental effects of industrial activity and innovation nationally and internationally.
- Risks and benefits.
- Regulations which control manufacturing, the transport and sale of products as well as the disposal of wastes: the need for controls and their effectiveness.
- Project management.
- Quality control with emphasis on the needs of customers. Systems of quality assurance. Reliability.
- Problems associated with providing stable employment and achieving profitability.

Decision making
- The role of scientists as expert advisers within organizations, in public inquiries and at law.
- The parts played by international organizations, national and local government, non-governmental organizations, professional bodies, pressure groups, the media and individuals in determining policy with respect to applications of science and technology.

- Practical work with a strong vocational bias. Practical work is not done to demonstrate the 'truth' of some principle learned in theory but to obtain results relevant to a problem or process which is used in real-world scientific analysis. Students develop a culture where it really matters that results are, because they have to stand up in court, for instance, or the diagnosis of disease is based on them.

- The freedom to stay with things which are going well and ditch or modify things which are going badly.

- Opportunities for group work offering mutual support and encouragement, and rich opportunities for peer group learning and development.

- The integration of both theory and practice from the separate academic 'subjects', reflecting the multidisciplinary nature of the scientific tasks to be done in industry and commerce.

- The wide range of assessment methods to credit a larger variety of student qualities, knowledge and skills than is possible through terminal examinations. The emphasis in assessment is on achievement and success, crediting all the things which a student can do.

- The use of a wide range of active teaching and learning strategies.

- Continuous feedback to students about their performance and progress.

- The opportunities to recover, repeat or resit parts of the course if something goes wrong.

The attitude of employers

It is clear that many of the positive features of vocational courses outlined above and built into the new GNVQ specifications, harmonize closely with the types of qualification which industry would like to see its young employees possess. According to the CBI, employers want qualifications which empower individuals and raise their aspirations. Such qualifications should:

- give individuals every chance to achieve, while still being challenged – one person's success must not be another person's failure

- focus on outcomes or competence, making clear what people actually learn and can do

- develop core, transferable skills such as communication, problem solving and personal skills – these are the essential skills which enable individuals to flourish in employment and continue learning as well as to manage their lives

- ensure breadth of knowledge and understanding as well as awareness of their limitations

- enable breadth of opportunity and progression – qualifications should open doors rather than close them.

A rationale for assignment-based learning

Learning science in context

The GNVQ specification encourages students to learn science in a vocational or applied context, rather than as an abstract body of knowledge. This implies that problems, contexts and scenarios come first, with students then finding out the scientific facts and principles which help them to find answers.

Putting the context first and mining the seams of scientific knowledge afterwards implies a change in attitude towards science itself. In the technological, design and socio-economic worlds, science is simply one input to be evaluated for solving the problem in hand. This is not the world of the basic research scientist, where the coherence and logic of a body of knowledge is paramount as the starting point for research to extend that knowledge.

The point is that while science is good at explaining and predicting natural phenomena in carefully controlled environments, once scientific knowledge is applied in the messier world of human concerns, it can no longer prescribe everything necessary for producing solutions to design or technical problems. In these conditions, scientific investigation and the application of textbook theory may have only limited power.

Numbers in the text refer to the bibliography at the end of this chapter.

Some of the implications of this change in attitude in one of the applications of science, physics for engineers, were set out recently by John Sparkes in an article, 'The nature of engineering and the physics it needs'[1] as follows.

- Physics for engineers can be simplified. Only those aspects relevant to design and engineering need be covered.

- Physical theory should be presented as a model not as the truth, because theory is seldom the whole truth for human problems and engineers have to match theoretical models to the problem in hand, usually by simplifying things. Engineers evolve 'rules of thumb', simplifications to mathematical equations. These are only approximations but for those who simply want to use the formulae in a practical context, this is of minor importance.

- Physics concepts should be related to the engineering solutions and creations that depend on them, rather than to physics experiments and bench-top demonstrations.

- Physics need only be developed as far as is necessary for a particular course in hand. For environmental engineering, for instance, descriptions of physical phenomena, rather than analysis and manipulation of them, may be all that is needed.

Sparkes also makes another key distinction between the attitudes of scientists compared with those of engineers and technologists.

> When tackling a problem, if there are insufficient data or understanding for a clear conclusion to be apparent, the inclination of most scientists is to postpone a decision on what to do until more data have been obtained or more research has been done.
>
> By contrast, engineers used to having to meet deadlines, learn to make decisions even when the information and theories are incomplete, bearing in mind that corrective decisions can often be made later if necessary. ... One of the lessons that experience teaches is that delay and the accumulation of more information are just as likely to complicate the decision as to reduce it to a clear conclusion.

In an interview conducted in 1993, the same point is made in a medical context by the distinguished virologist, David Tyrrell.

> I acquired a feeling for the inadequacies of science in the 'real' world when I ran the Infectious Disease Unit at the Clinical Research Centre, Northwick Park, and we used to go round the wards with trainee doctors and some scientists. We would talk about patients and have two conversations.
>
> The first conversation might be,
>
> 'Well, what's the diagnosis?'
>
> 'We don't actually know.'
>
> 'Have we done all the tests?'
>
> 'Yes and some of them turned out negative but we know that 30% of the people who have this disease – let's say its typhoid – won't actually have typhoid bacilli in their blood.'
>
> The fact that they are not there does not mean this is not a case of typhoid.
>
> 'So, what are we going to do?'
>
> 'We could do some more blood cultures.'
>
> 'How long will that take?'
>
> 'If we want to be sure, we ought to wait another week.'
>
> 'But this chap's got a swinging temperature and is looking worse, what are we going to do?'
>
> Obviously the best guess we can make is that he does have typhoid, so we give him the appropriate antibiotics.
>
> All of that is not based on real scientific evidence. But we could go back and talk about the same patient again as scientists and say, 'What do we actually know, can we look for antigens?' So there are two perspectives, and the one which matters to people who have to get on with the job is taking the scraps of inadequate evidence, putting them together and making a best guess. That is the necessary way of using science, which a pure scientist would say is inadequate. You are not actually dealing with things you have established. But if you wait until you have established them, the patient might be dead.

A culture of active learning

GNVQ forces science teaching to be student-centred and active because it demands student-generated evidence of achievement based on their own assignment work.

A 'student-centered' approach does not mean that there is no place for teaching methods such as lectures. Responding reflectively to a lecture can be a valuable method of active learning and lectures or whole-class lessons should not be completely abandoned, partly because they provide variety and partly because scene-setting or imparting essential basic information can still best be done this way.

In the book, *Active teaching and learning in science,*[2] active learning is said to take place when students:

- have personal involvement with their learning
- make decisions about the outcome of their work
- own their work
- test their own ideas
- plan and design their own experiments
- report their results to the rest of the class
- evaluate their results
- discuss and interact purposefully in groups
- reflect on the work they have done and reformulate their ideas.

It goes on to review the main differences between teacher and student-centred learning as in table 8.1.

Table 8.1

Teacher-centred learning is characterized by:	Student-centred learning is characterized by:
■ teacher exposition ■ accent on competition ■ whole-class teaching ■ teacher responsible for learning ■ teacher providing knowledge ■ students seen as empty vessels to be filled ■ subject knowledge valued ■ teacher-imposed discipline ■ teacher and student roles stressed ■ teacher decides curriculum ■ passive student roles ■ limited range of learning techniques	■ group work ■ accent on co-operation ■ resource-based learning ■ students take responsibility for learning ■ teacher is a guide ■ student ownership of ideas and work ■ process skills are valued ■ self-discipline ■ students seen as source of knowledge and ideas ■ students involved in curriculum planning ■ students actively involved in learning ■ wide range of learning techniques employed

Assignment-based and problem-based learning

The term 'assignment' has gained currency to describe the student-centred activities which should make up the bulk of a GNVQ learning programme.

In some programmes, an exercise occupying an hour or less of learning time is called an assignment. At the other extreme, an assignment might be an elaborate project drawing on material from several units occupying all a student's time for several weeks.

Many staff in GNVQ Science pilot schools and colleges feel that an assignment should consist of a linked series of tasks making up a project which allows students to learn much of the science and its context in one element. Designing a series of tasks which hang together to form a coherent assignment, while integrating core skills, is not easy. We hope that our published assignment collections will provide good examples, which can either be used as they are, modified to suit your tastes or act as models for assignments you will write yourself.

If assignment-based learning is defined in this way as a series of linked tasks which address some larger, overall issue or question, it is very similar to problem-based learning in higher education. Contributors to the book, *The challenge of problem-based learning,*[3] describe how problem-based methods evolved as a way for medical students to learn the science necessary to understand disease and its treatment. On problem-based programmes the basic sciences are not taught separately. Students learn aspects of science as and when they need it to solve problems which are devised round clinical scenarios. Science is deconstructed and re-assembled by the students in the context of their professional concerns as doctors training to treat patients.

The purist proponents of problem-based learning insist that problem-solving must occur in teams. The exercises are so elaborate, need so much background, and the time for tackling them is so short that co-operating in teams to learn from each other is the only sensible way for students to proceed. Problems are considered one at a time, allowing students to concentrate on them, rather than splitting their attention between several different themes, which happens when basic sciences are taught in separate academic disciplines. This means that specialist staff operate as consultants outside their traditional areas of expertise, on all aspects of the problem on which students are currently working.

It seems unlikely that a team approach to assignment topics will be a universal feature of GNVQ programmes. In some schools and colleges assignments are being tackled one at a time and all members of the course team, no matter what their discipline, act as consultants on the current project. The assignment is usually devised by the staff member whose experience comes nearest to the performance criteria and range described in the element which the assignment is designed to cover. A GNVQ programme based on these principles is described in the case study at a college in the North east in chapter 3.

Bear in mind the following points when designing assignments. No single assignment can have everything but in each assignment students might encounter one or two of the following features.

- Learning science in an applied or vocational context

- taking pride in obtaining accurate and reliable experimental results

- using problem-solving or scenario formats to co-ordinate learning tasks and activities

- drawing on frontier aspects of science or technology in some assignments while looking at more familiar areas in others

- doing flexible assignments so that they receive a great deal of guidance when they are done early in the programme, but much less later on as the work becomes more student-centred and eligible for grading at merit or distinction

- team-working, since so much employment now involves project teams and

- understanding the learning processes and the reasons for doing exercises.

This last point is critical and more is said about it in the following section.

Reflecting on learning

The FEU document, *Extending the curriculum*,[4] contains the statement, 'Students will learn through and by doing assignments – but they have to be taught how to do this'.

According to another FEU publication, *Learning by doing*,[5] experiential learning by doing assignments is only effective if students, by acquiring learning skills, reflect on what they are doing.

> It is not sufficient simply to have an experience in order to learn. Without reflecting upon this experience it may quickly be forgotten or its learning potential lost. It is from feelings and thoughts emerging from this reflection that generalizations or concepts can be generated. And it is generalizations which enable new situations to be tackled effectively.

This implies that students must understand how they are learning; they must be conscious of 'learning to learn'. Reflecting on how they are learning does not come naturally yet research shows that self-awareness about learning technique is one of the most valuable assets a student can acquire.

A survey by Geoff Haywood and Joan Solomon, *A preliminary study of post-16 science education*,[6] compared the learning experiences of A level and BTEC National Diploma students. The study showed that even in assignment-based BTEC programmes, many students were not self-aware about their learning techniques, and therefore not benefiting as much as they should from their programmes of study.

What exactly are learning skills? The list given in *Active teaching and learning approaches in science*,[2] includes the headings in table 8.2.

Table 8.2

Study skill	Relevance to science student
Organizational	Skills needed to manage time effectively both in the laboratory and at home
Communication	Skills needed to work effectively within groups, discuss ideas and present reports of investigations
Numerical	Skills needed to analyse data, use calculators and present results graphically
Research	Skills needed to make effective use of a wide variety of resources including teachers, libraries, videos, computers, television and radio
Investigation	Skills to enable students to plan, hypothesize and predict; design experiments and carry them out effectively and safely; draw inferences

Note that there is a close parallel between science learning skills and core skills specified in the GNVQ programme.

Table 8.3

Educational learning skills for science	Vocational core skills
Communication	Communication Working with others
Organization	Improving own learning and performance Application of number
Numerical	Problem solving Communication IT
Research/Investigation	Problem solving (+ experimentation, safety, etc.)

If we redefine vocational core skills as learning skills they should immediately be perceived as useful by students. Since core skills run throughout the GNVQ programme, the necessary self-conscious development of learning skills should be built in at the same time. It also provides another reason for a highly desirable feature of a good GNVQ programme: integration of core skills with vocational teaching.

Learning styles

Different individuals learn in different ways. They learn better with some tutors than others, using some learning techniques rather than others, and do better in some social and physical environments than others. The only way to allow for this is to make sure that programmes of GNVQ assignments use tasks with a diversity of learning strategies.

One starting point for thinking about learning styles is to recognize the three basic student approaches to learning described by Entwhistle in his essay, 'A model of the teaching-learning process',[7] (see table 8.4).

Table 8.4

A Deep approach	B Surface approach	C Strategic approach
■ Intention to understand ■ Vigorous interaction with content ■ Relate new ideas to previous knowledge ■ Relate concepts to everyday experience ■ Relate evidence to conclusions ■ Examine the logic of the argument ■ Comprehension learning ■ Operation learning	■ Intention to complete task requirements ■ Memorize information needed for assessments ■ Failure to distinguish principles from examples ■ Treat task as an external imposition ■ Focus on discrete elements without integration ■ Unreflectiveness about purpose or strategies	■ Intention to obtain highest possible grades ■ Organize time and distribute effort to greatest effect ■ Ensure conditions and materials for studying appropriate ■ Use previous exam papers to predict questions ■ Be alert to cues about marking schemes

Educationists hope that students will adopt the deep approach, with the inbuilt motivation to try to understand what they are learning in depth. However, experience tells us that many students adopt either the surface strategy (do what is necessary to survive) or the strategic strategy (manipulate the system to maximum advantage), treating the educational programme as an obstacle course to be negotiated with maximum success for minimum effort.

In theory, teacher-directed, end-test dominated, passive teaching programmes encourage strategies B and C (surface and strategic) while student-centred, problem-solving, active programmes should encourage strategy A (the desirable deep approach).

Michael Prosser, in 'The effects of cognitive structure and learning strategy on student achievement',[7] describes research which demonstrates that active, problem-based learning techniques in higher education do encourage students to adopt the deep approach. He compared student populations in two Australian medical schools, one using traditional teaching, the other using problem-based learning.

Adelaide medical school has a traditional intake group and educational programme, with pre-clinical and clinical sections of the course kept separate, heavy dependence on lectures, tutorials and traditional ward work, with end-of-course exams using objective tests. The other medical school, Newcastle, admits significant numbers of unconventionally qualified students and undertakes a curriculum based on confronting selected clinical problems which require students to acquire the relevant basic science, clinical skills and knowledge for themselves. Students work in small groups and on their own. Assessment is predominently by modified essay questions, ward observation, oral interviews and tests of ability to evaluate research papers.

Students at the two institutions were asked to evaluate themselves on a Learning Inventory which looked at different learning styles. The results showed that the Newcastle students scored themselves high on attitudes indicating a deep approach, while Adelaide students adopted strategies typical of the surface approach.

Learning style inventories

To derive maximum benefit from active learning, students should be self-aware about how they learn and their strengths and weaknesses as learners. It is also useful if staff have some idea of the preferred learning styles of their students. Psychologists have devised practical systems for classifying individual learning preferences. Some of these have been successful and are published.

There are differences between the systems but they identify similar variations in learning strategy. Individuals can diagnose their own learning styles by answering a series of structured questions. Unfortunately, many of the published sets of questions are from adult management training programmes and are not very appropriate for student use.

Few people fall clearly into one learning style category; they are usually mixtures of several styles, stronger in some, weaker in others. In many systems the mixed categorization can be visualized by a mapping procedure.

Knowledge of the whole range of categories allows staff and students to see that people learn in different ways and realize that when a topic needs to be learnt using a method incompatible with their own style, they need to make extra effort to compensate. It also helps in building effective peer-learning groups to be aware of the variety of learning styles present. This allows more efficient and rational allocation of learning tasks among group members.

Brief accounts of two learning style inventory systems are given below. The first, by Anthony Gregorc, has been used successfully by a pilot school during its induction programme to make students more self-aware about their own learning.

Gregorc's learning styles

Anthony Gregorc sorted the learning process into two stages, perception (taking in information) and ordering (how the information is sorted and processed). He split each of these processes into two extremes, creating a matrix of four basic groups.

Figure 8.1

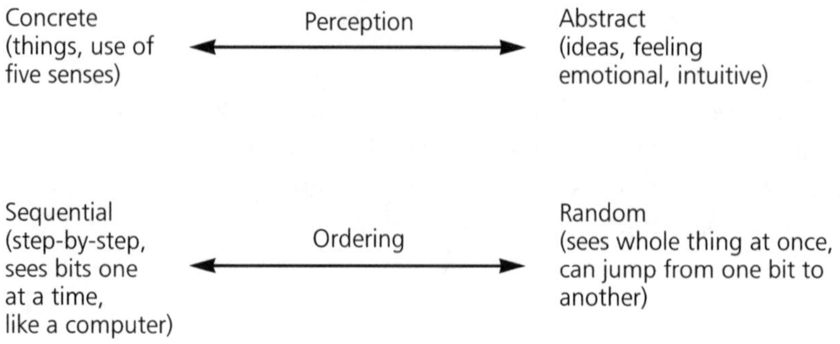

Concrete (things, use of five senses) ←— Perception —→ Abstract (ideas, feeling emotional, intuitive)

Sequential (step-by-step, sees bits one at a time, like a computer) ←— Ordering —→ Random (sees whole thing at once, can jump from one bit to another)

The four categories of people classified by learning style are therefore:

1 abstract sequential

2 abstract random

3 concrete sequential

4 concrete random.

To give some idea of the variations produced by classifying learning style in this way, consider some of the differences in learning behaviour characteristic of these groups.

Abstract sequential learners

- need to have concepts structured logically
- prefer to read, do research and use library
- need to be supported as thinkers
- find it difficult to articulate feelings
- don't like to express personal feelings
- like to work alone
- need time to think
- resist group work
- prefer bare work-spaces

Abstract random learners

- need to feel welcome in class
- thrive on personal attention, use of imagination
- work harder if: assignments involve other people, they have choices, there are reasonable deadlines
- can personalize and express their feelings
- easily upset
- like to relate to others

Concrete sequential learners

- need specifics, order and real problems
- facts, structures and practical details help them succeed
- find it easy to memorize
- find spelling easy
- have a head-start in objective tests

Concrete random learners

- need freedom to try, explore and mess with ideas
- work hard if not tied to someone's rules and if there are options
- creative – can see where things are going before they get there
- inventive, divergent thinkers
- questioning
- love starting, but not finishing

Figure 8.2

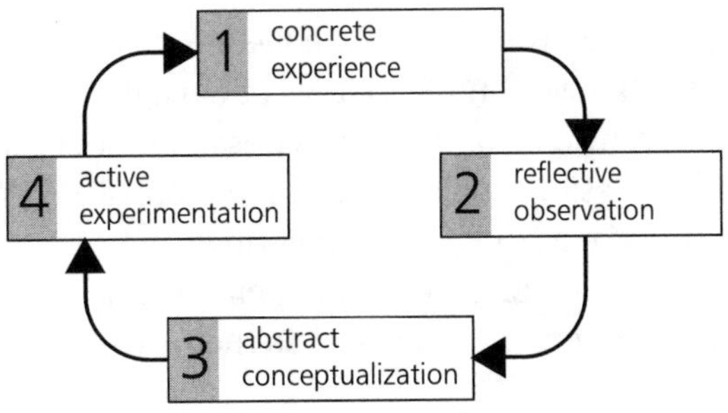

The Kolb learning cycle

David Kolb believes that experiential, active learning of the type advocated in assignment-based learning occurs in four stages in a cycle of learning experiences.

The learning process can begin at any point in the cycle but to be effective, the other three stages in the cycle must follow in sequence.

Psychological testing reveals that few people are equally facile at all stages in this cycle. Simple tests can show individual strengths and weaknesses. Kolb believes that people fall into four learning style categories, depending on which quadrant of the learning cycle is most comfortable for them, and he has explained this in the pamphlet, *Learning style inventory. Self-scoring test and interpretation booklet*[8].

```
1  concrete
   experience

4  active              2  reflective
   experimentation        observation

3  abstract
   conceptualization
```

Converger

Between abstract conceptualization and active experimentation. Greatest strength – the practical application of ideas.

Diverger

Between concrete experience and reflective observation. Greatest strength – imagination.

Assimilator

Between abstract conceptualization and reflective observation. Greatest strength – creating theoretical models.

Accommodator

Between concrete experience and active experimentation. Greatest strength – carrying out plans and experiments.

Another interpretation of strengths in the experiential cycle has been developed by Peter Honey and inventories and descriptions of the categories can be found in *The Manual of Learning Styles*[9].

Each style 'connects' with a stage on the continuous learning cycle. People with activist preferences are well equipped for 'experiencing'. Reflectors are suited to 'reviewing'. Theorists are well equipped for 'concluding' while those with pragmatist preferences are well equipped for 'planning'. Here are abstracts of Honey's descriptions of the types.

Activists

Activists involve themselves fully and without bias in new experiences. They are open minded and this makes them enthusiastic about anything new. They tend to act first and consider the consequences afterwards. They thrive on the challenge of new experiences but are bored with implementation. They are gregarious people but they seek to centre all activities around themselves.

Reflectors

Reflectors like to stand back to ponder experiences. They collect data and prefer to think about them thoroughly before coming to any conclusion. They postpone reaching definitive conclusions for as long as possible. They are thoughtful and like to consider all possible angles and implications before making a move. They prefer to take a back seat in meetings and discussion. When they act it is part of a wide picture which includes the past as well as the present and others' observations as well as their own.

Theorists

Theorists adapt and integrate observations into complex but logically sound theories. They think problems through in a vertical, step-by-step, logical way. They assimilate disparate facts with coherent theories. They like to analyse and synthesize. They are keen on basic assumptions, principles, theories, models and systems thinking. They tend to be detached, analytical and dedicated to rational objectivity.

Pragmatists

Pragmatists are keen on trying out ideas, theories and techniques to see if they work in practice. They positively search out new ideas and take the first opportunity to experiment with applications. They like to get on with things and act quickly and confidently on ideas that attract them. They are impatient with open-ended discussions. They are down-to-earth people who like making practical decisions and solving problems.

Team building

Peer group learning and some assignment-based learning requires students to operate in teams. Just as they need to be taught to reflect on their own learning to get the most out of active learning techniques, they also need to be taught about team dynamics and practise playing a variety of team roles to gain maximum benefit from learning in groups.

Because learning about team formation is central to much management training there are plenty of resources available for self-analysis. Unfortunately, as with some of the material for developing learning styles, it is not often entirely suitable for 16+ science students. One book which describes the basic mechanics of team building in a straightforward way is John Spencer and Adrian Pruss, *Managing your team. How to organise people for maximum results,*[10]. An article by Kate Douglas, 'Playtime for postgrads',[11] describes the programme of management team training run for postgraduate scientists by the Science and Engineering Research Council and gives similar information but in a setting a little closer to that of GNVQ learning.

Experts agree that an ideal team has individuals who fulfil certain stereotypical tasks (although there is considerable variation in the details of the various roles). Personality inventories can help individuals work out which roles most suit them. It is unlikely that any real team will have a correct balance of personalities. Therefore, team members may have to play against type and take on roles for which they are not ideally adapted. As with learning styles, the important thing is to be aware of your own strengths and weaknesses as a team player and to be aware of those of your fellow team members.

Kate Douglas suggests in her article that eight basic types are necessary to make a complete team. This draws on the classic work accessible in Belbin[13] and Johnson and Johnson[14].

Visionary

Team's vital spark and chief source of ideas. Creative, imaginative and unorthodox.

Co-ordinator

Team's natural chairperson and enabler. Mature, confident, clarifies goals, promotes decision-making.

Explorer

The team's fixer – extrovert, amiable, a wealth of contacts, explores options.

Shaper

Self-elected task leader. Dynamic, outgoing, highly strung, argumentative, pressurizer, seeks ways round obstacles.

Pragmatist

The team rock. Strategic, sober, introvert, discerning, capable of deep analysis of huge quantities of data.

Team-worker

Team's counsellor and conciliator. Perceptive, accomodating, promotes harmony.

Implementer

Team workhorse. Turns ideas into actions and gets on with them. Disciplined, reliable, conservative.

Complete finisher

Team worrier. Stickler for detail and deadlines. Chief catcher of errors and omissions.

Some pitfalls

In case you might be carried away by the new vision of enthusiastic, responsible students who take to active learning like ducks to water, here are some common pitfalls of experiential learning, taken from *Learning by doing – a guide to teaching and learning methods*,[12] by Graham Gibbs.

Here are some of the problems with experiential learning methods.

- Attempting too much – so allow plenty of time to set things up.
- Getting the balance wrong – so allow frequent opportunities for reflection.
- Assuming the learners are radical – so do not underestimate the importance of induction.

- Having no structure – so do not hesitate to give guidance especially during the early part of the programme.

- Over-planning and keeping too tightly to plan – so make sure that your students believe that their action planning is for real.

- Having no clear outcomes – so help students with their action planning and evaluation.

- Closing down options – so give scope for students to use their initiative as they must if they are to achieve merit or distinction awards.

- Undervaluing experience – so help students to see how their GNVQ studies build on what they already know and can do.

- Setting an unsuitable tone and atmosphere – so try to establish a non-threatening and supportive atmosphere.

- Not adjusting to the group – so make sure that induction is a two-way process and that students feel that they have a real say in the way their GNVQ runs.

Student-centred learning techniques are difficult to organize and time-consuming for staff to prepare but students who are encouraged to use them should be more effective learners in the end.

Bibliography

1 John Sparkes, 'The nature of engineering and the physics it needs', *Physics Education*, **28**, 1993, 293–6

2 Centre for Science Education, Sheffield Hallam University, *Active teaching and learning approaches in science*, Collins Educational, 1992

3 David Boud and Grahame Feletti (eds), *The challenge of problem-based learning*, Kogan Page, 1991

4 FEU, *Extending the curriculum*, 1986

5 FEU, *Learning by doing*, 1988

6 Geoff Haywood and Joan Solomon, *A preliminary study of post-16 science education*, Department of Education, Oxford University, 1993

7 Richardson, Eysenck and Piper (eds), *Student learning*, Open University Press, 1987: Entwhistle 'A model of the teaching-learning process', and Michael Prosser, 'The effects of cognitive structure and learning strategy on student achievment'

8 David Kolb, *Learning style inventory. Self-scoring test and interpretation booklet*, McBer, 1976

9 Peter Honey and Alan Mumford, *The Manual of Learning Styles*, Peter Honey, 1992

10 John Spencer and Adrian Pruss, *Managing your team. How to organise people for maximum results*, Judy Piatkus Publishers, 1992

11 Kate Douglas, 'Playtime for postgrads', *New Scientist*, 13 November 1993, 37–40

12 Graham Gibbs, *Learning by doing, a guide to teaching and learning methods*, FEU, 1987

13 R.M. Belbin, *Management Teams*, Heinemann, 1981

14 D. Johnson and F. Johnson, *Joining together: group theory and groups skills*, Prentice-Hall, 1982

Two case studies

We commissioned the two longer case studies in this chapter to complement the examples in chapters 3 to 6. Here you will find accounts of GNVQ Science in practice presented from the point of a sympathetic outsider. The studies include reflections on the strengths and weaknesses of GNVQ with discussion of useful lessons for newcomers to vocational science programmes. We have presented the general lessons first. The technical details of staffing, timetabling, course organization and assessment come towards the end to supplement the examples in earlier chapters. Both case studies end with hints for beginners.

CASE STUDY

GNVQ SCIENCE AT A COLLEGE IN THE NORTH

Context

The science department in this large FE College runs daytime and evening science A level and GCSE courses. Recently the BTEC National Diploma in Science has not been available. The department therefore chose to pilot GNVQ Advanced Science rather than revive BTEC National, and to pilot Intermediate level science as a replacement for GCSE dual award. The college offers GNVQs in most of the available areas.

GNVQ Science students

GNVQ Science has, so far, recruited from the 16–19 age group rather than adult students. Intermediate level has twelve students; Advanced began with nine, several of whom left during the first term. There are roughly equal numbers of boys and girls.

Intermediate level is open access. Careful counselling is provided by the student services department on application, and advice is given by the course team during induction. Access to Advanced level officially requires a BTEC First Diploma or four GCSEs at C or above, including C in separate or combined sciences. In practice these requirements have been eased a little in special cases. Two students initially admitted at Intermediate level were moved to Advanced level as a result of induction; one moved the other way. Only a few students are taking additional units.

Most students were recruited by word-of-mouth publicity. Perhaps for this reason, the provision of GNVQ Advanced does not appear to have affected A level numbers in the college.

Induction

Induction lasted just over two weeks, incorporating the college's one week common induction programme. Intermediate and Advanced students followed a joint programme to help students and staff with initial assessment: some intentions changed as a result. The focus was small ▼

▼ *continued from page 98*

assignments, set out as simulations of a GNVQ assignment but emphasizing the core skills and health and safety issues; one was an assignment on 'Finding out what the college has to offer you'; another was a 'social' assignment based on a visit to the Industrial Museum.

Students found the induction phase useful because it simulated the processes of the GNVQ course. Next year's induction is likely to simplify the arrangements further.

Teaching and learning arrangements

The approach to GNVQ builds on the 'BTEC style'. Learning is essentially assignment/activity led, with assignments and activities varying in size and scope according to the particular element/unit involved. Formal teacher input normally precedes assignments in order to establish the necessary knowledge and technique. Practical laboratory work is substantial; teachers keep students under deadline pressure in laboratory work to simulate the expectations in employment. Individual evidence collection consumes a significant amount of student time. Students are showing an increasing ability to use their own study time well, but limited access to laboratories is a problem: in some other GNVQ areas, independent work can be done in a variety of places; science is more limiting because of its laboratory demands and resource implications. GNVQ students occasionally 'drop in' to A level and Access laboratory times when there is room; this eases the problem but is not a generally satisfactory solution.

The implications of the pilot range statements, performance criteria and evidence indicators, taken together, create some difficulty for the course team. The work implied is substantial, as are the resource needs. It will not be possible to cover the full range through assignments; for testing purposes the gaps have to be filled in by didactic methods supported by internal 'mini-tests'. Even with this slimming down, teachers feel constrained by and restricted to the specifications: there is too little opportunity to develop students' conceptual frameworks, to stretch and extend understanding, and to follow open-ended ideas. The team is convinced that the range must be reduced.

Evidence is another concern of the team. It is not always practicable or appropriate – both in terms of the basic performance criteria and of the merit and distinction themes – to capture the quality of scientific achievement in permanent, documented form.

Employer links are proving difficult. The team decided not to use the facilities available in the college for organizing work placements, preferring to take responsibility themselves so that science activities could be incorporated into placements. This has proved an unrealistic ambition given the workload of a pilot year. But several industrial trips are planned, as is a work-based assignment. Given a longer 'lead time' next year, it should prove easier to tie employers in.

Staffing and timetabling

GNVQ advanced is taught by a team of one physicist, two chemists and one biologist. One of the chemists is timetabled to allow some interchange with another on the A level programme. The team for GNVQ intermediate is three of those teaching advanced (one chemist, one

▼
▼

chemist/biologist, and one chemist/physicist). Teacher adaptability, particularly across biology and chemistry, is seen as important, as is the small size of the team. Approximately half the team has chemistry knowledge, reflecting a response to the perceived emphasis of the early science specifications. Core-skills teaching is integrated.

One member of the team acts as course-team leader. This position carries no extra pay. A timetable remission of two hours is given, but in practice it averages about one hour over the year because of varying timetable and other constraints.

Timetable slots are college-determined to allow for additional units. Intermediate and Advanced levels receive the same allocation: 8×90 minute laboratory-based periods, blocked into two sessions on each of three mornings and one afternoon. Students have access to a further 5 hours of 'science workshop' time, staffed by a chemist and biologist with technician support; this is available jointly to Advanced and Intermediate level students, on one morning and one afternoon each week. The 17 hours of teaching are supplemented by a weekly one-hour group 'pastoral' session. There is a weekly one-hour Record of Achievement session, normally used for one-to-one work, for each of Intermediate and Advanced groups.

Student time therefore totals 18 hours, with additional one-to-one Record of Achievement sessions on occasions.

GNVQ Science students comprise one tutor group at each level for 'pastoral' provision. The physicist in the course team acts as tutor for Advanced level, a chemist for Intermediate.

Course organization

It is clear that mandatory units should be covered before optional units, to provide maximum opportunity for re-testing if necessary.

For Intermediate level, mandatory unit 1 runs throughout the year. Units 2 and 3 run in parallel during the autumn term, being tested in January. Unit 4 runs during the spring term (tested in May) in parallel with the first optional unit ('The nature of everyday change') taught largely by the chemist. The second optional unit ('Energy for people') is taught by the physics/biology staff in the summer term.

For Advanced level, unit 8 ('Data handling') pervades the course. Other units are planned to run in parallel pairs of a term each.

If a unit clearly identifies itself as essentially 'biology' or 'chemistry' or 'physics', it is taught primarily through that perspective. When it is false to separate into distinct sciences, the team aims for integration. This is particularly important in view of the initial staffing emphasis on chemistry. The course team maintains that the specifications of some units – particularly at Intermediate level – allow considerable flexibility to develop teaching programmes with contexts and emphases drawn from biology, chemistry or physics.

Clear separation between units is proving unrealistic: certain aspects of performance criteria and range in later units are covered by work in earlier ones; thus an accumulating 'internal' form of APL develops. Students are encouraged to claim, on the basis of current work, achievements that will carry forward to later units.

▼
▼

CASE STUDY

▼ *continued from page 100*

The team is finding significant imbalance between units – and elements of units – in terms of the demands made on students. This, and the preceding point, make it unlikely that a clean-cut 'two units per term' pattern will be sustained. This view is reinforced by the slow pace at the outset of the course. At Advanced level, GNVQ Science is demanding of students' laboratory techniques, which tends to slow down the pace of work. At Intermediate level many students arrive at college lacking much self-motivation, drive and organization so there is doubt about their ability to cope with the whole programme in a year.

The policy for core skills is to integrate them fully into vocational work, handled by science staff. A maths workshop is available to students who need it, and a specialist staff 'consultant' on each core skill area is available to science staff as necessary. The main difficulty of the integrated approach is shortage of convenient IT resources. Students' responsibility for claiming core skills is given prominence. Indications of likely core skills are included on assignment cover sheets. The team hopes that later in the course it will be possible to omit these, with students expected to take the initiative to identify and claim achievement.

Assessment, record keeping and testing

BTEC was chosen as the awarding body, both for its general and science reputation and for its kudos in higher education. The college submission, being started late, was very demanding. Most of the support and staff development has been found within the college rather than from the awarding body. The college is an accredited centre for TDLB awards: most staff are already part of D32/D33 training.

The team's assessment and record keeping system has several components.

For each major assignment, project or report, the student receives a *guidance sheet* indicating assignment title, unit, elements, names of first and second line assessors, start date and deadline date, plus the relevant vocational and core-skills performance criteria. Attached to the sheet is an outline of the context of the work, the tasks involved – including indications of which parts relate to specific vocational and core-skills performance criteria – and guidance with compiling the evidence.

This guidance is supported by a *student assessment record sheet*. For each assignment, this lists each applicable performance criterion, summarizes the nature of the evidence, and identifies relevant page references in the portfolio. It includes a section for possible grading evidence. Once signed by the assessor, the completed sheet is kept by the student, while a copy stays in the course team's records. Students retain their portfolios, so this acts as a partial safeguard against portfolio loss.

An overview of evidence is maintained with the *evidence cross-reference grid* – a matrix indicating performance criteria for vocational units against activity numbers – and the *location of evidence sheet*. Using this sheet, the student maintains, for each vocational and core skill unit, a record identifying each element, referencing it to activity numbers and portfolio page numbers.

The teacher responsible for a particular assignment is 'first line' assessor for it, making initial assessment of all students. Another member of the team acts as 'second line' assessor, sampling three students for each ▼

assignment. The internal verifier samples three, including one that has received 'second line' assessment. Two science staff currently handle D34 internal verification, one of whom also teaches on another GNVQ course. All stages in this process are documented. An external verifier, who is a scientist, has been appointed and has visited within the first term.

Essential advice for those starting GNVQ Science

Only through designing and preparing assignments do teachers come to understand the possibilities and limitations hiding within the formal specifications. Thus the first year or two are bound to be tentative and exploratory in approach, subject to considerable revision.

Use the BTEC not the A level approach. If you don't have recent BTEC experience, talk to and learn from colleagues who are used to this style of work; this will help when planning assignments.

Particularly at Advanced level, students must be self-motivated: the ones that aren't will drop by the wayside – carefully-planned induction activities, with plenty of practical science activity early on rather than too much theory, will do most to encourage self-motivation.

Become quickly familiar with core skills, especially the different levels and the range statements. Adapt the normal induction programme so that students are also covering core skills using induction assignments.

Staff training on documentation for assessing, for tracking and for portfolio-management is vital, as is planning for, and making all staff aware of, the storage system for assessment documents.

CASE STUDY

GNVQ SCIENCE AT A SCHOOL IN THE NORTH

Context

A Grant Maintained, 13–18 mixed comprehensive in a northern city, the school has over 1200 on roll, with 330 sixth form students. Complementing a good range of A level courses, its GNVQ provision covers Intermediate and Advanced in Business and Health and social care, and Intermediate in Art and design and Leisure and tourism. It is a pilot school for Advanced GNVQ Science. GNVQ is seen as important to the sixth form programme, so tackling science at the earliest opportunity was a natural choice.

GNVQ Science students

Eleven boys and three girls, whose overall GCSE attainment is generally in the C/D range, are taking the course. A condition of entry was at least a C in the NEAB co-ordinated science. Three in the group had already done one 'unsuccessful' year of A level science, and one student had done two.

CASE STUDY

▼ *continued from page 102*

Advanced GNVQ Science was promoted positively as an appropriate alternative to struggling with A level, and as offering a different – possibly more appropriate – style of learning and method of assessment. By mid-November, there were no 'drop-outs' and the team leader was optimistic that all fourteen students would stay the course.

Induction

The planned four-week induction phase was conceived as an introduction for students to the GNVQ ethos and method. Its main objectives were to develop student responsibility for learning and assessment, to encourage student management of planning and recording systems, to establish the significance of core skills, to model the method of work in and outside class, and to foster the relationship of student and teacher.

To tackle these objectives, the team developed an 'invented' unit, with suitable elements, range, performance criteria and evidence indicators, including core skills. The full timetable with all four staff was devoted to activities and assignments for this 'unit'. The simulation lacked only formal GNVQ assessment and a test. The teachers deliberately 'stood back a bit'.

Reflecting on the experience, the team remains satisfied that the purpose was sound. But the quality of work was not as good as they had hoped. Students found difficulty with the concepts in the unit; were sometimes frustrated by practical and equipment problems; and found the relatively loose structure, combined with the level of responsibility required, quite taxing. The induction phase over-ran, with knock-on effects.

Next time, the basic idea will be retained, with certain changes in method. There will be a definite four-week limit, using a more straightforward simulated unit containing tasks designed for quick success and accomplishment. The team will provide more structure and greater teacher intervention to set and assure positive standards of work.

Teaching and learning arrangements

Each 'theme' is presented in one or more student booklets. 'Assignments' are defined as 'jobs to be done'. Students work through a series of assignments, many of limited extent, designed to build up the necessary underpinning knowledge across the range. Mostly these are not subject to assessment. Practical work is included among the assignments. These normally culminate in a more substantial integrative report, project or write-up of the topic concerned. This contains the assessment evidence for the student portfolio.

Student quality influences the teaching approach. The usual range of methods is employed; but teachers are finding that they need a direct approach to the acquisition and understanding of underpinning knowledge. This is because the previous attainments, experience and motivation of the group are mixed. It is proving harder and slower than hoped to achieve the shift from teacher-dependency and low work-rate; the peer culture tends to counter self-motivation, self-reliance and sustained hard work.

While that is the view from the GNVQ teachers' perspective, the Head of sixth form observes that the GNVQ Science students appear to be doing ▼ more work in private study time than the generality of A level students. ▼

This could be attributed to the greater level of information, guidance and monitoring that their work is receiving. The different perceptions of the teachers and of the Head of sixth form may also have something to do with the fact that the GNVQ philosophy and structure implicitly raise teachers' expectations of how students ought to work: does it reveal (and therefore potentially tackle) problems that with A level tend to remain conveniently hidden?

Some special equipment has been purchased for the course, and some additional investment made in library resources. In general, the staff find that a judicious use of existing GCSE and A level texts, supplemented by newspaper and similar sources, is satisfactory for GNVQ. Resource constraints should not prevent a school offering GNVQ science: the unit specifications enable the devising of assignments to suit existing resources.

Links with employers are not at present built into the work. The school has good employer links, and one of the biologists is the school's work experience officer, but so far the need for industrial links has not been felt.

Staffing and timetabling

The course team consists of a physicist, two biologists and a chemist. One teacher of English, one of maths, and one of IT, are responsible for core skills. The physicist acts as course-team leader, without an additional responsibility allowance or remission of teaching time.

The school operates a day of seven 40 minute periods. All GNVQ Science teaching occurs in double-period sessions. Core-skills workshops receive a single period for Communication and for Application of number, and a double for IT. The students have 13.3 hours of class time on vocational units and 2.6 hours for core skills workshops: a total of 15.9 hours of contact time.

GNVQ Science students (with a few from GNVQ Business) comprise one tutor group for 'pastoral' matters; the science course-team leader acts as form tutor.

Course organization

The staff define the vocational flavour of their GNVQ approach as taking science not as an end in itself, but in the context of real world situations. The aim is to help students to think scientifically while handling science with a technological bent: practical and experimental work is thought of in terms of actual problems and applications, the testing out of hypotheses, and the recognition of uncertainty and error.

In planning the programme, the course team for the Advanced GNVQ decided that all but one of the mandatory units have a particular emphasis. They saw units 1, 3 and 6 as essentially chemical; units 2 and 5 as essentially physical; units 4 and 7 as essentially biological. Unit 8 was regarded as pervasive: a view reinforced by NCVQ's choice of unit 8 as the one to be omitted from testing.

The team planned year 12 to cover, and tackle tests on, mandatory units 1, 2, 3, 4, 5 and 7 – two for each 'subject' focus. Year 13 would be for mandatory unit 6, consolidating mandatory unit 8, and covering the four optional units. Student and staff numbers mean that students will not ▼ ▼

▼ *continued from page 104*

have any choice of optional units, which will be those chosen by the school.

As an organizing framework, each 'subject' pair of units is linked more or less loosely under a theme: The car (2 and 5); Human biology, Biotechnology, Ecology (4 and 7); The chemical industry; Further chemistry (1 and 3). These themes are arranged into (mostly) five-week time blocks. In any time block students follow two themes.

Planning on pilot schemes is not an exact science. Events have gone more slowly than the team anticipated, the timescale 'slipping' by at least two weeks in the first term. So, if the tests are to be taken when planned, not all of the range will have been completed through assignment work. The 'slippage' was caused partly by the induction phase lasting until half term, and partly by the time taken over practical work: the students enrolled are those who would have found difficulty with A level, and their relatively weak practical skills have tended to slow things down.

One consequence of the chosen course structure is that, except for the 'biological' units, students are often working on a unit with a non-specialist. This creates some obvious difficulties. But the likelihood of being able to staff every part of a GNVQ Science programme with a specialist at all times is so remote that the difficulties have to be lived with and tackled.

The assumption that pilot unit 8 can be diffused throughout the other units is proving not wholly valid. Element 2, in particular, contains mathematical concepts and methods that do not fit naturally into the other units or easily into many science teachers' expertise, so it needs some specialized maths input.

Core-skills workshops are timetabled with specialists. Workshops are mostly exclusive to the science students, though a few from other GNVQ programmes are timetabled into workshops with the scientists, while some tend to miss out initially because of GCSE resit timetable conflicts. For 'application of number', the teacher is trying to tailor work to the units on which students are currently working, while IT and 'communication' are more self-contained. Core-skills assessment is carried out by vocational unit teachers as far as possible; core-skills teachers may have to provide some supporting opportunities for assessment of certain performance criteria.

Assessment, record keeping and testing

The school uses RSA as its awarding body for science – though it works also with BTEC and City and Guilds for other GNVQs. The team has devised its own adaptations of formats suggested by the awarding bodies. The assessment and record keeping system rests on several documents.

A *Unit logbook* summarizes the elements, performance criteria, and range of the unit. It contains a matrix showing PCs against assignment numbers, and includes a form giving assignment number, details, start and target dates, with space for staff comment. Space is also available for dates and results of unit tests, enabling staff and students to 'sign off' the unit when fully completed. A *Unit portfolio key* lists each of the performance criteria, with space for identifying evidence and giving a portfolio reference code.

▼
▼

For each major project or report, students receive a *guidance sheet* outlining the task, including indications of which parts relate to specific vocational and core-skills performance criteria. This is supplemented by a *planning sheet* summarizing the activity, identifying the vocational and core-skills elements covered, and indicating types of possible evidence, including that for grading. On the reverse is a *review sheet* which allows assessors to indicate completion or omissions in relation to the evidence.

Students are required to annotate their reports and projects with code numbers, in a different colour, to indicate evidence for claiming achievement in specific performance criteria.

The GNVQ co-ordinator, a senior teacher, works closely with the internal verifier (also assistant Head of sixth form and a member of the core-skills team) who at present covers the school's full range of GNVQ courses. Two of the science team are currently acquiring D32/D33. The school is experiencing the widespread uncertainty about the role of internal and external verifiers in relation to specialist knowledge: can they 'verify' procedures without 'moderating' performance standards? On the answer to that question depends the staff structure adopted for assessment and verification.

Essential advice for those starting GNVQ Science

Plan assessment first! GNVQ is assessment-led, differing fundamentally from A level and significantly from BTEC National in this respect. Do not start out with fine ideas for 'content' and for learning activities without being sure that these will enable students to develop and collect appropriate evidence for assessment.

Small is best! The smaller a course team can be, consistent with adequate breadth of expertise, the better: the coherence of GNVQ experience for students depends on tight liaison across the team.

Remember tutoring! The timetable allocations in this pilot year did not allow for tutorial support sessions; such support is very important.

Planning has many facets! Two of the teacher team were on maternity leave during the first term of the pilot phase…

Resources

Nuffield Science in Practice began in September 1992 and since then we have been collecting a library of resources relevant to vocational courses. We have also gathered ideas from pilot centres. We have reviewed the resources with GNVQ in mind and added brief comments in the tables below.

Please note that this is not a definitive or complete list but we know that many centres have found it helpful as a starting point for building up a bank of resources. You will find a list of addresses for all but the major publishers at the end of this section.

We cannot quarantee that the items listed below are still available or in print. A few of the packs are very expensive with prices up to £100, but generally we have tried to keep to items that are more modestly priced.

Once the final GNVQ specification is available, we will be able to match resources to the units, elements and performance criteria. We will publish the results of this exercise in our files of assignments.

GNVQ management and assessment

Details of resource	Notes and comments	GNVQ level
The GNVQ Staff Development pack from the Walsall Metropolitan Education Committee TVEI team: *Senior Management Perspective, Middle Management Perspective, The Assessor Tutor* and *Working with other Agencies*.	A series of guides written to cover all GNVQs. Useful for pointing up issues affecting all GNVQ programmes in a centre.	Intermediate/ advanced

Learning and teaching styles

Details of the resource	Notes and comments
Peter Honey and Alan Mumford, *The manual of learning styles*, 1992. ISBN: 0 9508444 7 0 and Peter Honey, *Using your learning styles*, 1986. ISBN: 0 9508444 1	Student-centred learning approaches require students to learn through a wide range of techniques and to reflect actively on how they are learning. One approach to student learning styles has been Kolb's experiential learning cycles. These have been developed extensively in the worlds of industrial training and this book discusses these styles and provides self-assessment questionnaires.
Centre for Science Education, Sheffield City Polytechnic, *Active teaching and learning approaches in science*, Collins Educational, 1992. ISBN: 000 327829 8	A book aimed at active learning in the National Curriculum. Everything is also relevant to post-16 education, especially to GNVQ. There are 16 chapters on different active learning techniques followed by a series of examples of active learning exercises. Permission to photocopy them for classroom use is granted. Many of these would be useful as they stand or with modification for the induction phases of a GNVQ programme.
Phil Race, *53 interesting ways to write open learning materials*, Technical and Educational Services Ltd., 1992. ISBN: 0 947885 60 9	One of a range of books advising beginners on how to set about writing their own resources or to prepare study guides to help students learn from existing resources.
Philip Waterhouse, *Flexible learning. An outline*, Network Educational Press, 1990. ISBN: 1 85539 003 5 Robert Powell, *Resources for flexible learning*, Network Educational Press, 1991. ISBN: 1 85539 005 1	Two books from a series introducing the goals and methods of flexible learning.
David Boud and Grahame Feletti (eds), *The Challenge of Problem Based Learning*, Kogan Page, 1991. ISBN: 0 74940 249 0	A book which brings together examples of problem based learning at university level from many countries with case studies in medicine, architecture, computer studies, social work and other fields. The thesis is that students learn best when actively involved and learn in the context in which the knowledge is to be used.
Graham Gibbs, *Developing teaching: teaching more students 5 - Independent learning with more students*, PCFC, 1992	One of a set of booklets providing advice and exercises for HE teachers faced with growing student numbers. Some exercises might be adapted for use with GNVQ.

Core skills

Resources which cover a range of core skills

Details of the resource	Notes and comments	GNVQ level
The skills profile, CRAC/Hobson's, 1992. ISBN: 1 85324 666 2	Designed for KS4 in the National Curriculum, the exercises explore students strengths, weaknesses, attainments and competencies. Useful material for induction stage action planning. Permission to photocopy for classroom use is granted.	Intermediate
Ruraplan, CRAC/Hobson's, 1988. ISBN: 1 85324 082 6	A role-playing game about economic development in a rural community in which environmental problems are central.	Intermediate
The Metal Box business game and *Metal Box business game, extra dimensions*, CRAC/Hobson's, 1984 and 1989. ISBN: 0186021 646 2 (manual); Ref. No. 3 000000 406 (Manual and Disk) and ISBN: 1 85324 1881	A role-playing game for sixth-formers in which they learn some of the principles of managing a productive business.	Advanced
Tony Crowley, *The occupational interests explorer*, CRAC/Hobson's, 1989. ISBN: 1 85324 195 4	A set of questionnaires and interpretations to allow students to assess the employment area to which they might be most suited.	Intermediate/ advanced
Sue Habeshaw, Trevor Habeshaw and Graham Gibbs, *53 interesting things to do in your seminars and tutorials*, Technical and Educational Services Ltd, 1992. ISBN: 0 947885 08 0	Student-centred learning in science means that seminars and tutorials ought to play a greater role in teaching. This useful book gives guidance and ideas on how to organize and get the best value from these methods.	Intermediate/ advanced
Russell Ball and Glenn Archer, *Integrated science assignments, communication and IT skills*, Cambridge University Press, 1991. ISBN: 0 521 38728 0	Designed primarily for BTEC Science programmes, these exercises could be modified to fit components of GNVQ Science and core skills units. Background data and full laboratory schedules are included. Permission to photocopy for classroom use is granted.	Intermediate/ advanced

Details of the resource	Notes and comments	GNVQ level
William Bolton and Albert Clyde, *Training for the future*, Further Education Unit, 1990. ISBN: 1 85338 199 3	A group of 23 assignment ideas developed to explore interdisciplinary themes round the notion of 'key technologies', nodal areas in technology where developments will lead to problem solution and innovation in a wide range of application areas. Science and core skills are developed. Permission to photocopy for classroom use is granted.	Advanced
Albert Clyde, *Getting to grips with education and training for industry. A development of the concept of key technologies*, Further Education Unit, 1992. ISBN: 1 85383 271 X	A short manual in which the key technologies idea, around which the assignments above are based, is developed. Permission to photocopy for classroom use is granted.	Intermediate/ advanced
Simon Bysshe, *People and Medicine, a cross-curricular resource pack for secondary schools*, The Wellcome Foundation Ltd., 1993	A series of seven short exercises on themes of disease and the role of the pharmaceutical industry in combating it. Each one has some potential for core-skills development and the whole series together might make the basis of an assignment. Permission to photocopy for classroom use is granted.	Intermediate
BTA Study Cards from the British Trades Alphabet	A series of information cards presenting themes about British business, trade and industry. Intended for use with the national Curriculum and with the potential to provide a context for core skill activities in GNVQ science.	Intermediate

Communication skills

Details of the resource	Notes and comments	GNVQ level
Janet Bond, Chris Davenport and Brian Ford, *Core studies and Common skills*, CRAC/Hobson's, 1989. ISBN: 1 85324 237 3	A set of 200 tasks and assignments asking students to explore their attitudes to a variety of themes, providing opportunities for developing communication skills. Permission to photocopy for classroom use is granted.	Intermediate
Sue Habeshaw and Di Steeds, *53 interesting communication exercises for science students*, Technical and Educational Services Ltd, 1987, ISBN: 0 947 885 20 X	A series of ideas for working communication skills into science teaching programmes. Many of the examples can be used or adapted for core-skills work in GNVQ Science and as exercises in induction programmes.	Intermediate/ advanced
Newspapers in education: The newspaper activity book, The Newspaper Society, 1985. ISBN: 0 947906 02 9	A series of suggestions of how to use newspapers in the classroom to deal with topics in various disciplines, including science and technology. Designed for schoolchildren of all ages. Permission to photocopy for classroom use is granted.	Intermediate
A communication skills package for use in HE physics departments, Institute of Physics, 1992	This large package was assembled to provide a framework for developing communication skills among physics undergraduates. However, a great deal of the material would be useful for exploring aspects of core communication skill. A number of debate simulations and team building games are included which would be invaluable in building group and team skills. Permission is granted to photocopy for classroom use.	Advanced
The *On Target* series and the *Innovation file* from MBA Publishing	Files of industrial case studies with suggested activities mailed free to schools. Intended mainly for business studies but providing industrial and technical contexts for cores skills in science.	Intermediate

Information technology

Details of the resource	Notes and comments	GNVQ level
Steve Kennewell, Peter Fox, Chris Mitton and Ian Selwood, *Computer studies through applications*, Oxford University Press, 1992. ISBN: 0 19 8327633	A well produced book designed for GCSE Computer Studies but the content and suggested assignment ideas are adaptable to GNVQ. The principles of computing are taught through analysis of real-world industrial, commercial and public-sector problems.	Intermediate
Michael Hammond, *Handling data with databases and spreadsheets - a classroom pack*, Hodder and Stoughton, 1993. ISBN: 0 340 58971 X	A series of exercises for introducing and practising data handling on computers. Several of the exercises have a scientific or environmental base and could prove useful to integrate into GNVQ assignments to improve IT skills. Permission to copy students sheets for classroom use is granted.	Intermediate/ advanced
Peter Creese and Ken Webster, *Global information system. SatCom satellite simulator*, World Wide Fund for Nature, 1993. ISBN: 0 947613 92 7	This is an information system for schools on environment/ development issues. Software which will run on most school computers feeds in data from a series of satellites hovering over the Earth, monitoring various environmental parameters. A series of exercises and activities are then built round this data, covering elements of IT, communication, science and technology in KS 3 and 4 of the National Curriculum. There is a wealth of data which could be built into assignments. Permission to photocopy for classroom use is granted.	Intermediate
David Squires (ed), *Newsnet*, British Telecom and Computers in the Curriculum. n/d	This pack contain software, background booklets, Teachers' Guide and User's Guide for a computer networking exercise in which news stories are gathered, edited and laid out on the front page of a newspaper. Several of the stories have a scientific or environmental bias. Originally designed for KS3 pupils, the exercise has been used successfully with KS4 and post-16 students. The GNVQ core skills of IT and communication are covered in this package. Permission to photocopy for classroom use is granted.	Intermediate
John Layman and Wendy Hall (Co-ordinators), *A town like Wattville, a computer simulation of electricity use in a town*, Understanding Electricity Educational Service, 1989	This package contains computer software and full colour teacher and student guidance sheets for a set of exercises on the supply of electricity to a small town. These were designed as cross-curricular exercises for the National Curriculum and relate particularly to IT, mathematics and science with some geography and home economics. They could be adapted for assignment work in GNVQ, with considerable scope for integrating all the core skills.	Intermediate
Practical Science with Microcomputers, National Council for educational Technology, 1990. ISBN: 1 85379 114 8	A set of photocopiable activity sheets designed for use with the science National Curriculum at Key stages 3 and 4. Intended to support the use of the Sense and Control data logger. Perhaps too tightly structured for direct application in GNVQ.	Intermediate
National Environmental Database Project, *Animal Ecology, Radioactivity, Acid Rain*, Technical manual, Kings College, London	Three potential assignments with details of practical techniques and a national database for exchanging data with other centres.	Intermediate/ advanced
Scottish Power, *Domestic electricity*, 1992.	Designed for KS 4. Three programmes allow students to investigate energy consumption in the home. Students can calculate power, cost, and energy used by switching appliances on and off and discover the benefits of white-meter, off-peak tariffs.	Intermediate
John Layman and Wendy Hall (Co-ordinators), *Power Control, a computer simulation of power station operations*, Understanding Electricity Educational Service, 1988	This package contains computer software and full colour teacher and student guidance sheets for a set of exercises on power generation and control, comparing coal, oil, pumped-storage and nuclear power plants. The principles of how all these station types work are explained. Considerable scope for integrating all the core skills.	Intermediate
Telecom Link. A game for sixth-formers, Institute of Electrical Engineers and British Telecommunications plc, 1991 and *Link-up: A scientific simulation exercise*, Institute of Electrical Engineers, 1992	These are two variations of the same theme, a decision-making game about building a new telecommunications link between London and Amsterdam. The main point of the exercise is to decide between three or four technical solutions to the problem. Students group into teams representing firms bidding for the contract, each using a different technology. The contract is awarded to the 'best' bid. Full instructions and background technical data are supplied. Permission to photocopy for classroom use is granted.	Intermediate/ advanced
D. Squires (ed) and A. Edis (programmer), *Pulse code modulation*, British Telecom Education Service, n/d	A pack designed to look at the science and technology of encoding analogue signals into digital pulse chains. It contains a teacher's book, software and a student guide to its use in a number of exercises and simulations. It was originally designed for GCSE and A level electronics syllabuses.	Advanced

Application of number

Details of the resource	Notes and comments	GNVQ level
Jon Ogborn and Dick Boohan (eds), *Making sense of data. The Nuffield exploratory skills data project*, Longman, 1991. ISBN: 0 582 07361 8	Nine cased booklets, each containing 'real-world' exercises in data-handling and analysis. It might provide a source from which to develop assignments and provide examples of raw data. It is expensive (£85.00 + VAT).	Intermediate/ advanced
Dorothy Coates and Glen Cormode, *Newspapers in education: newspapers and mathematics*, The Newspaper Society, n/d. ISBN: 0 94790607 X	A series of suggestions and workcards for using newspapers as a resource for teaching mathematics. A small number of these relate specifically to scientific or technical issues.	Intermediate

Personal skills and problem solving

Details of the resource	Notes and comments	GNVQ level
David Wright (Project Director), *Solving problems past-16*, ASE, Employment Department, 1992. ISBN: 0 86357 164 6	A guide to using problem-solving activities as teaching/learning methods, together with a bank of 80 problems and 25 detailed action sheets. Permission to photocopy for classroom use is granted. Some of these exercises could provide the basis for assignment design and others are useful for induction.	Intermediate/ advanced
Durham University Business School, British Steel Industry, *Enterprise. An educational resource for 14–19 year olds*. Casdec Ltd., 1991. ISBN: 0 948608 78 1	A collection of four modules (Asking questions, Finding ideas, Making plans and Producing results) about solving technical problems in a business context. These could be used in isolation or together to provide ideas for assignments with an emphasis on business enterprise. Individual sub-components could be used as short exercises, especially for developing things like team-building in induction programmes. Permission to photocopy for classroom use is granted.	Intermediate/ advanced
Durham University Business School, British Steel Industry, *Enterprise in vocational education and training, skills development*, Business Education Publishers Ltd, n/d	A pack designed to foster 'business enterprise' skills across the whole curriculum. Since these overlap significantly with core and learning skills and one section focuses on electronics, there are potential ideas and data for assignment design. Alternatively, individual exercises could be lifted out and used for induction or to cover elements of core skills. Permission to photocopy for classroom use is granted.	Intermediate/ advanced
R.K. Pegg, *The curriculum enrichment programme, start-up pack, 'Developing skills for a working life'*, University of Liverpool, 1992	A pack designed to foster self-development and core skills and attitudes in the widest sense. Team-work is a special focus. Therefore, there are many exercises and ideas which could be adapted to deal with core skills in a vocational context. Several of the project briefs deal with applied scientific areas such as computer interfacing, chemical synthesis and protecting the environment. These might provide a basis for assignment design.	Intermediate/ advanced
Rachel Hudson, *Write your own cv*, CRAC/Hobson's, 1989. ISBN: 1 85324 212 8	A self-learning programme for enhancing success in job applications.	Intermediate/ advanced
Alan Paull, *The application game*, CRAC/Hobson's, 1989. ISBN: 1 85324 248 9	A role-playing game in which sixth-formers learn about the pleasures and pitfalls of applying for a place in HE.	Advanced
Unilever plc, *Stance, a role-playing business exercise*, Unilever Educational Liaison, 1990. ISBN: 0 9035440 08	Students form teams of six which take on separate managerial roles in a company making liquid detergent products. Each team is then presented with up to 10 issues upon which a management decision must be taken. Students work first on their own, arriving at a decision on an issue in the light of the role they are playing. Then they have to negotiate with the other managers in their team to arrive at a decision. Several of the issues, such as Health and Safety, introducing New Technology and Production Quality are directly relevant to GNVQ Science units, while the others are useful for background work on business decision making. The exercise is also good for developing a wide range of communication skills. Permission to photocopy for classroom use is granted.	Intermediate/ advanced
M. Robson, *Problem Solving in Groups*, Gower Publishing Company Ltd, 1993. ISBN: 0 566 07415 X	A source of ideas for training in team work and problem solving derived from management training.	Intermediate/ advanced
J. Spencer and A. Pruss, *Managing Your Team - how to organise people for maximum results*, Judy Piatkus Publishers Ltd, 1992. ISBN: 0 7499 1295 2	A source of ideas for training in team building. Includes some exercises which could be adapted for GNVQ.	Intermediate/ advanced

Publications which include science activities/assignments

Resources which cover a range of science applications and issues

Details of the resource	Notes and comments	GNVQ level
Nuffield Modular Sciences, Pathways through Science, Longman (1992–4). Thirteen modules: *Bodywise, Chemicals, Control and Communication, Earth and atmosphere, Electricity, Energy resources, Environment, Forces, Making materials, Materials, New life, Plants and animals, Radiation*	The modules cover the Key stage 4 programme of study. Each module has a pack of photocopiable of activities. Many activities link both to the science units in GNVQ and to core skills. The Sourcebooks which accompany the modules feature many people who use science in their work.	Intermediate
Wessex Study Guides for students: *Aspects of Ecology, Aspects of Inheritance, Astronomy, Automation, Biotechnology, Catalysts and Catalysis, Clothing from Natural Materials, Drugs, Medicines and People, Electricity for the Future, Energy for Living, Forensic Science, Investigating Perception, Making Polymers for a Purpose, Medical Physics, Mechanical Properties of Materials, Nature and Action of Drugs, Radioactivity in Use, Separation and Purification, Sound Reproduction, Structural Materials, Telecommunications*, Wessex Publications, 1993	A wealth of flexible learning materials written for A-level science courses but adaptable for GNVQ. Some modules assume prior knowledge from the A-level core. In places the language is at a high level – especially for students near the start of the course.	Advanced
Ken Austwick and Eon Harper (eds), *Working Science*, Cambridge University Press, 1991. ISBN: 0 521 39821 5	A set of student-centred exercises in which school science and technology are placed in industrial contexts. Some of the exercises contain practical work, for which full protocols are given. Many of these could provide the basis for assignments in GNVQ Science. Permission to photocopy for classroom use is granted.	Intermediate
Bill Harrison (Project Director), *Problem solving with industry. A resource to support the teaching and learning of science and technology in Key Stages 3 and 4*, Sheffield City Polytechnic, Centre for Science Education, 1990–1992	A series of four booklets of scientific problem-solving exercises based on industrial contexts. On occasion, the scenarios seem a little contrived. Permission to photocopy for classroom use is granted.	Intermediate
Brian Nicholl and Jenny Selfe (eds), *Experimenting with industry*, SCSST and ASE, 1985	A series of 14 booklets, each sponsored by a different company in separate industrial sectors, containing a series of experiments which can be done in school laboratories and are relevant to industrial practice and industrial problem-solving.	Intermediate/ advanced
S.T.E.E.L. (Science, Technology and Engineering Education in Lancashire), Science and Industry publications, 1978–82	A series of practical exercises based on scientific and technical procedures which are carried out in industry. The techniques can be carried out in school and college laboratories and the industrial background could be developed into assignments. Titles still available include; Fungal growth in emulsion paint, Use of the Roche 'Enterotube' system in microbiology, The Preparation of Chloral, Chloral hydrate and DDT, The recovery of silver from photographic waste, Bacterial control in the food industry, Material science in the paper and plastics industries, Use of volumetric analysis in the chemical industry, Safe canning, Some applications of GCSE physics in testing and processing textiles.	Intermediate
David Andrews, *Science, Technology and Society*, Stanley Thornes Limited, 1992. ISBN: 0 7487 1293 3	A photocopiable resource pack containing a large collection of relatively short activities designed for General Studies and related courses. Topics include: IT, the Reproduction Revolution, Medicine Health and Society, A Pill for Every Ill, Energy – resources and consumption also nuclear power.	Intermediate/ advanced

Details of the resource	Notes and comments	GNVQ level
Twelve SATIS (Science and Technology in Society) booklets and an Update book, Association for Science Education, 1986–1991	Each booklet contains ten short photocopiable units illustrating applications of science or issues related to science and technology in society. Designed as 'infusion' units for GCSE science. Each unit has activities for students. The scheme as a whole covers a very wide range of topics.	Intermediate
Four SATIS 16–19 files from the Association for Science Education, 1990–1992	Each file contains 25 photocopiable units. Some support general education, others are more specialized. Each unit has notes for guidance, a study guide, information and a commentary. Many can be a good basis for intermediate and advanced assignments. Many of the units feature activities which support the development of core skills.	Intermediate/ advanced
Joan Solomon, *What is Science?*, (ISBN: 0 86357 158 1) *What is Technology?* (ISBN: 0 86357 159 X) and *How does Society decide?* (ISBN: 0 86357 160 3)in the SATIS 16–19 series, Association for Science Education, 1992	Three short readers which provide a framework for selecting and using photocopiable units form the four SATIS 16–19 files. Pitched at advanced level.	Advanced
ODA, *Science in Action – Aid and the Developing World*, Association for Science Education	A video in three parts with associated photocopiable activity sheets. Designed to complement the Science National Curriculum. Might be adapted for intermediate level. The section on the cold chain in China has a technological approach. The other two sections deal with biogas and the armyworm as a pest.	Intermediate
Peter Chamberlain (ed) TASTE packages, 1990, now available from the Association for Science Education. Titles: *Medicines, Testing Medicines, Domestic Energy, Thermal Images, Brewing, Bar Codes, Communications, The Firbeck Factor*	These packages were developed by TASTE as a Joint Support Activity in Barking, Dagenham, Havering, Newham and Redbridge. The packages were designed to make links with local industry. Intended for use in the National Curriculum. All feature opportunities for group learning, problem solving and open-ended tasks.	Intermediate

Biotechnology and microbiology

Details of the resource	Notes and comments	GNVQ level
Biotechnology in practice, Hobson's Scientific, 1990. ISBN: 1 85324 315 9	A set of 21 practical exercises and supporting information together with teacher's notes and bibliography. Permission to photocopy for classroom use is granted.	Intermediate/ advanced
Practical biotechnology, a guide for schools and colleges, AFRC and National Centre for Biotechnology Education, 1993	A pack of 23 practical biotechnology exercises connected with agriculture and food. A source book of themes for assignments with detailed practical protocols. All the procedures have been successfully trialled in school laboratories. Permission to photocopy for classroom use is granted.	Intermediate/ advanced
National Centre for Biotechnology Education, *Dairy biotechnology*, National Dairy Council, n/d	A pack consisting of pupils' guides, teacher's notes and sets of assignment sheets for 10 practical exercises. Designed for KS 3 and 4 of National Curriculum, the material seems entirely suitable for science GNVQ, and not only at intermediate level.	Intermediate/ advanced
SSCR Biotechnology Group, *Biotech*, Association for Science Education, 1987. ISBN: 0 86357 057 7	Five pretty substantial photocopiable SATIS-style assignments with a good variety of activities. Intended for GCSE. Lots of opportunities to develop core skills.	Intermediate
Peter Freeland, *Investigations in applied biology and biotechnology*, Hodder and Stoughton, 1990. ISBN: 0 340 50630 X. Also in the same series is Peter Freeland, *Micro-organisms in action; investigations*, ISBN: 0 340 53922 4	A series of practical investigation exercises set in the form of short problems to be solved. All are integrated into an applied context. Full practical protocols are given together with teacher's and pupil's notes. Permission to photocopy the student sheets for classroom use is granted.	Intermediate/ advanced
Paul Wymer, *Practical Microbiology and Biotechnology for Schools*, Macdonald Educational, in Association with the Microbiology in Schools Advisory Committee, 1987	An authoritative guide with 30 suggested activities. The pack consists of a Teachers' Guide with photocopiable workcards.	Intermediate/ advanced
Stephen Tomkins, Michael Reiss and Christine Morris, *Biology at work*, Cambridge University Press, 1993. ISBN: 0 521 38962 3	A traditional textbook which considers biology solely in terms of its applications. A valuable sourcebook for data and assignment ideas.	Advanced

Applied chemistry

Details of the resource	Notes and comments	GNVQ level
Karen Davies (compiler), John Johnston and Neville Reed (eds), *In search of solutions. Some ideas for chemical egg races and other problem-solving activities in chemistry*, Royal Society of Chemistry, 1990. ISBN: 1 870343 15 8	A series of practical exercises in the form of problems. Full basic documentation and practical protocols are provided. Permission to photocopy for classroom use is granted. The book is aimed at the National Curriculum but a fair number of exercises are suitable for 16+.	Intermediate or induction
George Marchant and Bob Mudd, *Post-16 chemistry activities*, Wessex Publications, 1993	A set of 33 assignments/activities originally designed for teaching a common programme of A level and BTEC National Diploma courses at Gloucestershire College of Arts and Technology. Permission to photocopy for classroom use is granted.	Advanced
Making use of science and technology, Chemical Industry Education Centre. Example, War against pests, 1992. ISBN: 1 85342 510 9	A series of packs containing guidance booklets and student work material on chemistry in industry and the environment. Practical and active learning techniques are emphasised. Designed for use at KS 3 and 4. Assignments could be based on this material. Permission to photocopy for classroom use is granted.	Intermediate
Nuffield Advanced Chemistry, *Special Studies*, Longman 1984	Topics in applied chemistry (with practical activities): Food Science, Biotechnology, Chemical Engineering, Metals as Materials, Mineral Process Chemistry, Surface Chemistry.	Advanced
Salters Advanced Chemistry, *Storylines* and *Activity Pack*, Heinemann, 1994. ISBN: 0 435 631063/0 435 631071	Many ideas which can be adapted to cover aspects of the advanced units as well as giving opportunities to developing core skills in a chemistry context.	Advanced
Chemistry case studies, City of Sheffield Education Committee and Sheffield Regional Centre for Science and Technology, 1983	A series of case study books of chemical production processes and pollution control with data drawn from the Staveley Chemical Plant. Science and technology in both its industrial and wider social context. They are not currently in an active learning or problem-solving format.	Intermediate/ advanced
Peter Tooley, *An Introduction to Chemical Techniques and Experiments in Applied Chemistry*, John Murray, 1975	Out of print but might suggest ideas. Full practical details are included.	Advanced
David Edwards and David Waddington (ed), *Chemistry in Action*, University of York Science Education Group and Granada Television, 1987. ISBN: 0 904005 06 2	Ten teaching units illustrating social, industrial and economic aspects of chemistry. Linked to Granada videos. Teachers' Guide and photocopiable activity sheets. Intended for GCSE.	Intermediate
Ben Faust (compiler), John Johnston and Neville Reed (eds), *Modern chemical techniques*, Royal Society of Chemistry, 1992. ISBN: 1 870343 19 0	The principles of a series of modern analytical techniques are set out. Each chapter also carries a group of interpretative exercises. Permission to photocopy for classroom use is granted. This is a valuable source book for assignments and problem-solving exercises.	Advanced
The Earth's resources, metals, RTZ Corporation plc. n/d	A pack of five sets of activities built round five themes to do with exploring for, mining, transporting and using metals, employing RTZ data and experience. This could provide a model for building useful educational links with local firms.	Intermediate
Decisions with industry, RTZ Corporation plc. n/d	A series of 4 packs looking at a different issue in the production process. Teacher guides and student sheets are included in each one. Active learning techniques are used where possible. A certain amount of 'real-world' materials science is covered. Permission to photocopy for classroom use is granted.	Intermediate
S.W. Breuer, *The Importance of Shapeliness*, Lancaster Science and Technology Pamphlets, 1989. ISBN: 0 901 272 67 1	One of a series of short booklets written for post-16 students with information, case studies and exercises. There are four biology volumes in the series related to genetics, ecology and the circulatory system.	Advanced
J.E.D. Davies, *Structure Determination Using Molecular Spectroscopy*, Lancaster Science and Technology Pamphlets, 1989. ISBN: 0 901 272 68 X	A short booklet written for post-16 students with information, case studies and exercises.	Advanced
The essential chemical industry, The Chemical Industry Education Centre, University of York, 1989. ISBN: 1 85342 500 1	A reference book of industrial data about chemical compounds which play a large role in the chemical industry. Valuable source of information and data about applied chemistry for assignment design. Permission to photocopy for classroom use is granted.	Intermediate/ advanced

Applied physics

Details of the resource	Notes and comments	GNVQ level
Physics in Engineering Project, *Mechanics and Heat*, Cambridge, 1992. ISBN: 0 521 36676 3	One of a series of books which emphasises the practical uses of physics in industry and engineering. Contains data from authentic applications. Lots of problems and exercises.	Advanced
Physics in Engineering Project, *Electricity*, Cambridge, 1992. ISBN: 0 521 36677 1	One of a series of books which emphasises the practical uses of physics in industry and engineering. Contains data form authentic applications. Lots of problems and exercises.	Advanced
David Sang and Robert Hutchings, *Energy*, Macmillan, 1991. ISBN: 0 333 531 09 4 (Part of the Bath 16–19 Project now published by Nelson.)	Aimed to cover A-level energy resources options. Covers energy resources, thermodynamics, and transport. Includes short assignments, problems and questions.	Advanced
P.K. Tao, *The Physics of Traffic Accident Investigations*, Oxford University Press, 1987	Lots of interesting data and case studies. See also a related SATIS 16–19 unit.	Advanced
Martin Hollins, *Medical Physics*, Macmillan, 1990. ISBN: 0 333 466 57 8 (Part of the Bath 16–19 Project now published by Nelson.)	Aimed to cover A-level medical physics options. Covers human mechanics, senses, biomedical measurements, the uses of ionizing radiations and radionuclides. Includes short assignments, problems and questions. The book ends with a major case study simulating the uses of medical imaging in a hospital.	Advanced
David Sang, *Nuclear Physics*, Macmillan, 1990. ISBN: 333 466 58 6 (Part of the Bath 16–19 Project now published by Nelson.)	Aimed to cover A-level nuclear physics options. Covers atomic structure, nuclear processes and nuclear technology. Includes short assignments, problems and questions.	Advanced

Environmental topics and issues

Details of the resource	Notes and comments	GNVQ level
Bob Campbell, Sylvia Hogarth and Robin Millar (eds), *Teaching and learning about the environment*, University of York Science Education Group, 1991. ISBN: 0 86357 150 6 (Available from ASE)	A series of practical and active learning exercises on scientific issues connected with the environment. The pack contains excellent material on science in its broader social context and could develop GNVQ core skills. Permission to photocopy for classroom use is granted.	Intermediate/ advanced
John Pickup and Chris Meddle, *Issues, trouble with algae*, Hobson's Scientific, 1992. ISBN: 1 85324 579 8	One of a series of magazine style presentations of issues in which scientific and technical phenomena present social and economic dilemmas. The exercises are designed to allow students to see how to make up their own minds as informed citizens about these issues. Activities and data are built in and it might provide a basis for GNVQ assignment design.	Intermediate/ advanced
Rachel Bennington, *The greenhouse effect teaching pack*, National Society for Clean Air and Protection, n/d	A series of information and assignment sheets encouraging active learning on this well-worn theme. Permission to photocopy for classroom use is granted.	Intermediate
Acid rain teaching pack, National Society for Clean Air and protection, 1992	A series of information and assignment sheets encouraging active learning on this second, well-worn environmental theme. Permission to photocopy for classroom use is granted.	Intermediate/ advanced
Ken Webster, science booklet in *The Decade of Destruction, the Story of the Amazonian Rainforest during the 1980s*, WWF, 1991. ISBN: 0 947613 31 5	Designed for use in the National Curriculum at Key stage 3 the complete resource consists of a video linked to comprehensive teaching/learning materials for Geography, Science and English. Topics covered include mining, mineral processing, metal extraction and the environmental impact of exploiting natural resources. Could be adapted for intermediate level with the video and a number of photocopiable newspaper articles being used as the primary source material. Opportunities for communication skill activities.	Intermediate
BBC, *The Global Environment*, BBC Educational Publishing, 1990. ISBN: 0 563 34696 9	A series of broadcast programmes available on video with booklet of photocopiable activities. Covers the environmental implications of using energy resources, raw materials and water. Intended for KS 3 in science and geography but the videos are certainly suitable for older students.	Intermediate

Details of the resource	Notes and comments	GNVQ level
Helen Springall *et al, Nitrates – environment and health*, Field Studies Council, 1991. ISBN: 1 85153 823 2	The basis of an assignment involving monitoring using test strips. Link to data disc so IT possibilities too.	Intermediate
Ken Webster, *Energy - economic awareness and environmental education*, WWF UK, 1990. ISBN: 0 947613 16 1	A collection of nine units about Energy issues with photocopiable activity sheets, information sheets and data sheets. Intended for use with the National Curriculum in science and maths. Could be adapted to support the core skill numeracy.	Intermediate
Cherry Mares (ed), *Waste issues*, The Tidy Britain Group, 1990. ISBN: 0 905277 13 9	A pack containing background notes and students project sheets for an exercises in the practical problems of waste disposal and management. Group work is encouraged and basic science and core skills issues can be explored.	Intermediate
Waste management and resources, The Tidy Britain Group. n/d	A practical science unit, designed originally for KS 4, which helps pupils to understand the relevance of science and the environmental impact of society. The pack looks at how the quality of the environment is affected by the production, consumption and disposal of goods.	Intermediate
W.A.H. Scott, *Safe for the future, Radioactive Waste Educational Project for the 14–19 Curriculum*, UK Nirex	A problem solving simulation which might be adapted for intermediate level. Information cards give basic background information. The resource is photocopiable for use in school.	Intermediate

Food and nutrition

Details of the resource	Notes and comments	GNVQ level
Thorburn Kirkpatrick, *The most useful science. Chemical and biological science in the future's food industry*, Northern Foods, 1988. ISBN: 0 947707 03 4	A booklet containing a series of 29 experiments related to scientific work in the food technology industry, set in a background account of the gamut of available foodstuffs and some scientific data about them.	Advanced
Eon Harper Consultants, *Milk break two. Vital vitamins*, National Dairy Council, 1990	Teacher's guide and assignment sheets for an exercise in the discovery of vitamins and their occurrence and stability in milk. Designed for the National Curriculum. Permission to photocopy for classroom use is granted.	Intermediate
Deanna Clarke and Marilyn Watte, *The human machine, a project for secondary schools*, The Butter Council, n/d	A pack containing a series of work cards and teacher information sheet on the themes of food, digestion and nutrition. Individual, group and practical activities are built into the material. Permission to photocopy for classroom use is granted.	Intermediate
Jill Davies and John Dickerson, *Nutrient Content of Food Portions*, The Royal Society of Chemistry, 1991. ISBN: 0 85186 426 0	A compilation of accessible tables for analysing the nutrient content of diets and menus. Based on standard portions rather than the amounts (RDAs) and weights of food consumed. Linked to UK recommended daily amounts (RDAs) and healthy eating guidelines.	Intermediate/ advanced

Genetics

Details of the resource	Notes and comments	GNVQ level
Wilbert Garvin and Dr Lorraine Stefani, *Genethics (Genetic disease and ethics)*, Northern Ireland Centre for School Biosciences, The Queens University, Belfast, 1992	A role-play exercise designed for students who already have some knowledge and understanding of Mendelian genetics. The role play features Cystic fibrosis, Duchenne muscular dystrophy and Huntington's disease. The published material includes guidance for teachers, role cards and worksheets.	Intermediate/ advanced

Human physiology, health and performance

Details of the resource	Notes and comments	GNVQ level
Juliet Crooks, *A-level Study Notebooks*, Haldon Publications, 1992	A set of A-level Study Notebooks for Human Biology – matched to the AEB syllabus. Could be useful in establishing basic coverage of range.	Advanced
Alastair Campbell and Roger Higgs, *In that Case*, Darton, Longman and Todd, 1982. ISBN: 0 232 51557 3	Case studies with exercises for discussion. Written for doctors, nurses, community and social workers and health visitors.	Advanced
King Edward Hospital Fund for London, *The Nation's Health – a strategy for the 1990s*, 1989. ISBN: 1 85551 038 3	Lots of data about health and disease.	Advanced
Roy Hawkey, *Sport Science*, Hodder and Stoughton, 1991. ISBN: 0 340 52523 1	Covers physical science aspects of sports science as well as applied biology.	Intermediate
Peter Freeland, *Sports Science – a project pack for GCSE and standard grade*, Educational Project Resources	A series of cards with information, questions and practical activities about the human form, physiology, diet, nutrition and fitness.	Intermediate

Materials science

Details of the resource	Notes and comments	GNVQ level
Enterprising technology, BP Education Service, 1991	A pack designed for National Curriculum KS 4 Technology, making special use of BP's expertise in plastics. The possibilities for using a variety of plastics to produce a series of products to meet market needs are analysed (including sport, catering, healthcare and fibres and textiles) with the aim of teaching some principles of business enterprise. Permission to photocopy for classroom use is granted.	Intermediate
Paper, glass, metals, plastics, The Tidy Britain Group n/d	Four practical science units, designed originally for KS 4, which help pupils to understand the relevance of science. The pack looks at the properties of materials and how the quality of the environment is affected by the production, consumption and disposal of goods.	Intermediate
Which materials?, Institute of Materials, 1990	A set of introductory case studies in the problems of finding the right material to meet specific industrial needs.	Intermediate
Brian Cooke and David Sang, *Physics of Materials – for A-level students*, The University of Leeds, 1986. ISBN: 0 904421 15 5	Written for A-level students faced with new topics coming into advanced level syllabuses. Includes discussion questions, problems and other activities.	Advanced

Plants and animals

Details of the resource	Notes and comments	GNVQ level
Eve Gillman (ed), *The milk business*, National Dairy Council, 1992	A series of sixteen linked assignments collected on four themes (the milk round, Oak Valley Farm, consumer tastes and Potter's Dairy), designed to interact with a wide range of subjects in the National Curriculum. The exercises have some value for GNVQ core skills development and the sections on farming and dairy production could stimulate science assignments.	Intermediate
W.A.H. Scott, *Feed the world*, British Agrochemicals Association, n/d. from Educational Project Resources	A series of activity sheets looking at food production and the threats to it on a global scale. Science and core skills could be developed with this material. Permission to photocopy for class use is granted.	Intermediate
Peter Freeland, *Habitats and environments; investigations*, Hodder and Stoughton, ISBN: 0 340 554339	A series of practical investigation exercises set in the form of short problems to be solved. All are integrated into an applied context. Full practical protocols are given together with teacher's and pupil's notes. Permission to photocopy the student sheets for classroom use is granted.	Intermediate/ advanced
Urban Ecology Study Unit, *The freshwater ecology pack*, Hodder and Stoughton, ISBN: 0 7131 7633 4 (Also of interest is: *The woodland ecology pack*, ISBN: 0 7131 7634 2)	Originally designed for pre-16 pupils, this material could be adapted for GNVQ. The pack consists of a Teachers' Guide, a set of instructions for 9 fieldwork techniques (mainly biological and physical) and a series of investigations together with some identification keys. Permission to photocopy for class use is granted.	Intermediate

Details of the resource	Notes and comments	GNVQ level
Hilary Thomas, *Investigating chalk grassland, a resource for investigations in schools*, White Cliffs Countryside Project, Kent Trust for Nature Conservation, 1991	A pack for students to investigate the value of chalk grassland as a wildlife habitat using a range of skills, a case study, secondary sources of information, fieldwork and research. They produce a report on the development and management of a hypothetical area of chalk downland. Designed for pupils at KS 3 and 4. Permission to copy for classroom use is granted.	Intermediate/advanced
Newsletters from Science and Plants for Schools (SAPS) – also fast-plant kits now becoming available from Philip Harris.	SAPS Newsletters are a rich source of ideas for investigations. SAPS has developed kits for investigations with 'fast-plants' (rapid cycling brassicas) which make it possible to carry through genetics and other studies with plants in a manageable time.	Intermediate/advanced
Ian Brodue and Julian Doboski, *Techniques in Ecology and Environmental Science*, Daniels Publishing, 1991	An excellent source of data and techniques for ecological tasks and assignments.	Advanced
Neil Chalmers *et. al., The Open University Project Guide to Fieldwork and Statistics for Ecological Projects*, Open University Press, 1986	An excellent source of data and information on techniques.	Advanced

Telecommunications

Details of the resource	Notes and comments	GNVQ level
John Price Consultants, *Designing a telephone. A technology resource for 14–16 year-olds*, British Telecommunications, 1993	A very flexible resource (including the 'innards' of a telephone) for technology which could perhaps be adapted to science programmes. Since it is very deliberately aimed at the 14–16 age group, it might need disguising before use with post-16 groups. Permission to photocopy for classroom use is granted.	Intermediate
Ray Walker, *Electricity and Telecommunications, 16 Worksheets*, British Telecom Education Service, 1991. ISBN: 0 948 257 78 4	A lively set of worksheets covering elements of physics and electronics, generally in an applied context. Designed as lesson supplementation for National Curriculum teaching. Permission to photocopy for classroom use is granted.	Intermediate
Sean Lawlor, *Getting the message. Communications guide for teachers and students*, British Telecom Education Service, n/d	This pack is designed with GCSE Technology at KS 4 mainly in mind. Two detailed data books and several pamphlets are provided as background material for a series of activity sheets. Permission to photocopy for classroom use is granted.	Intermediate
NS Educational Consultants, *Project: Earth Station. Technology and the environment*, Field Studies Council and British Telecom, n/d	A pack with 20 colour slides and detailed data sheets which uses satellite monitoring and communication as a theme around which to build role-playing exercises on the impact of technology on the environment. Individual slide/data sheets can be used in isolation for smaller exercises with a science content. Designed as a cross-curricular project for KS 3 and 4 of the National Curriculum, the whole or parts could be adapted to GNVQ Science where it would accentuate core skills. Permission to photocopy for classroom use is granted.	Intermediate
John Allen, *Telecommunications*, Macmillan, 1990. ISBN: 0 333 47627 1 (Part of the Bath 16–19 Project now published by Nelson.)	Aimed to cover A-level telecommunications options. Covers radio, satellites and fibre optics. Includes short assignments, problems and questions.	Advanced

Addresses (other than major publishers)

This list gives the addresses for suppliers of resources referred to in the tables above.

Ashgate Publishing Ltd, Gower House, Croft Road, Aldershot, Hants GU11 3HR

Association for Science Education (ASE), College Lane, Hatfield, Hertfordshire AL10 9AA

The British Agrochemicals Association, 4 Lincoln Court, Lincoln Road, Peterborough, PE1 2RP

Association of the British Pharmaceutical Industry, 12 Whitehall, London SW1A 2DY

BNFL Education Unit, Risley, Warrington, Cheshire WA3 6AS

BP Educational Service, Brittanic House, 1 Finsbury Circus, London EC2M 7BA

British Organ Donor Society, BODY, Balsham, Cambridge CB1 6DL

British Steel Education Service, PO Box 10, Wetherby LS23 7EL

Business Education Publishers Ltd., Leighton House, 10 Grange Crescent, Stockton Road, Sunderland, Tyne and Wear SR2 7BN

BT Education Service, British Telecommunications plc, 81 Newgate Street, London EC1A 7AJ

British Gas, Education Liaison Officer, Room 707A, 326 High Holborn, London WC1V 7PT (for information)

British Gas Education, PO Box 70, Wetherby, West Yorkshire LS23 7EA
(For resources)

British Trades Alphabet, PO Box 32, Thames View Business Centre, Thames View, Abingdon, Oxfordshire OX14 3LJ

The Butter Council, Tubs Hill House, London Road, Sevenoaks, Kent TN13 1BL

Casdec Ltd., 22 Harraton Terrace, Birtley, Chester-le-Street, County Durham DH3 2QG

Centre for Research Education and Training in Energy (CREATE), Kenley House, 25 Bridgeman Terrace, Wigan WN1 1SY

Centre for Science Education, School of Science, Sheffield Hallam University, 36 Collegiate Crescent, Sheffield S10 2BP

Chemical Industry Education Centre, Department of Chemistry, University of York, Heslington, York YO1 5DD

Chichester Press Ltd, PO Box 110, Chichester, West Sussex PO19 2HG

Colour Museum (Curator), 82 Grattan Road, Bradford BD1 2JB

The Conservation Trust, George Palmer Site, Northumberland Avenue, Reading RG2 7PW

Council for Educational Technology (CET), 3 Devonshire Street, London W1N 2BA

Daniels Publishing, Barton, Cambridge CB3 7BB

East Midlands Electricity (Marketing Services), 398 Coppice Road, Arnold, Nottingham NG5 7HX

Educational Project Resources, Freepost, London SW7 4YY

Eurotunnel Exhibition Centre, St. Martin's Plain, Cheriton High Street, Folkestone, Kent CT19 4QD

Further Education Unit (FEU), Information Centre, 2 Orange Street, London WC2H 7WE

Hobsons Publishing plc, Bateman Road, Cambridge CB2 1LZ

Peter Honey, Ardingly House, 10 Linden Avenue, Maidenhead, Berks SL6 6HB

Institute of Electrical Engineers (Schools, Education and Liaison) Michael Faraday House, Six Hills Way, Stevenage, Herts, SG1 2AY

The Institute of Food Science and Technology, 5 Cambridge Court, 210 Shepherd's Bush Road, London W6 7NL

Institute of Metals, 1 Carlton House Terrace, London SW1Y 5AF

Institute of Physics, IOP Publishing, Techno House, Redcliffe Way, Bristol BS1 6NX

King's College London, Centre for Educational Studies (NED Project) London SW10 0UA

MBA Publishing Ltd, PO Box 5, Wetherby, West Yorkshire LS23 7EH

The Met. Office Education Service, Johnson House, London Road, Bracknell, Berkshire RG12 2SY

National Council for Educational Technology (NCET), Sir William Lyons Road, University of Warwick Science Park, Coventry CV4 7EZ

National Centre for Biotechnology Education, Department of Microbiology, University of Reading, Whiteknights, Reading RG6 2AJ

The National Dairy Council, 5-7 John Princes Street, London W1M 0AP

National Extension College, 18 Brooklands Avenue, Cambridge CB2 2HN

National Society for Clean Air and Protection, 136 North Street, Brighton, East Sussex BN1 1RG

Network Educational Press (NEP), Network House, PO Box 635, Stafford ST17 0JR

The Newspaper Society, Bloomsbury House, Bloomsbury Square, 74-77 Great Russell Street, London WC1B 3DA

Northern Foods plc. Beverley House, St. Stephen's Square, Hull HU1 3XG

R.K. Pegg, Project Director, University of Liverpool, Curriculum Enrichment Programme, 14 Oxford Street, PO Box 147, Liverpool L69 3BX

RSPCA Education Department, Causeway, Horsham, West Sussex RH12 1HG

RTZ Educational Resources for Schools, Intermail Ltd, 10 Fleming Road, Newbury, Berks RG13 2DE

Science and Plants for Schools (SAPS), Homerton College, Hills Road, Cambridge CB2 2PH

Scottish Power, Public Affairs Dept., Cathcart House, Spean Street, Glasgow G44 4BE

Speak out and Listen, PO Box 7, Winchcombe, Cheltenham GL54 5HY

The Standing Conference on Schools' science and technology, 1 Birdcage Walk, London SW1H 9JJ

S.T.E.E.L. Woodlands in-Service and Conference Centre, Southport Road, Chorley PR7 1QR

Technical and Educational Services Ltd., 37 Ravenswood Road, Bristol BS6 6BW

The Royal Society of Chemistry, Turpins Transactions Limited, Blackhorse Road, Letchworth, Herts SG6 1HN

The Tidy Britain Group, The Pier, Wigan WN3 4EX

UK Nirex, Information Office, Curie Avenue, Harwell, Didcot, Oxon OX11 0RH

Understanding Electricity Education Service, 30 Millbank, London SW1P 4RD

Unilever Educational Liaison, PO Box 68, Unilever House, London EC4P 4BQ

Walsall TVEI Centre, EDC, Field Road, Bloxwich, West Midlands WS3 3JF

The Wellcome Foundation Ltd., Community Relations Executive, PO Box 129, 160 Euston Road, London NW1 2BP

Wessex Publications, Elwell House, Stocklinch, Ilminster, Somerset TA19 9JF

WWF UK (World Wide Fund for Nature), Panda House, Weyside Park, Godalming, Surrey GU7 1XR